Journey to a
Brave New World,
Part Two

Journey to a
Brave New World,
Part Two

US Civilian Labor Camps, the Trojan Horse
for the Communist Takeover of the United
States, and a Plan to Stop It

David Watts

iUniverse, Inc.
Bloomington

JOURNEY TO A BRAVE NEW WORLD, PART TWO
US Civilian Labor Camps, the Trojan Horse for the Communist Takeover of the United States, and a Plan to Stop It

iUniverse books may be ordered through booksellers or by contacting:

iUniverse
1663 Liberty Drive
Bloomington, IN 47403
www.iuniverse.com
1-800-Authors (1-800-288-4677)

Because of the dynamic nature of the Internet, any web addresses or links contained in this book may have changed since publication and may no longer be valid. The views expressed in this work are solely those of the author and do not necessarily reflect the views of the publisher, and the publisher hereby disclaims any responsibility for them.

Any people depicted in stock imagery provided by Thinkstock are models, and such images are being used for illustrative purposes only.
Certain stock imagery © Thinkstock.

ISBN: 978-1-4759-9189-5 (sc)
ISBN: 978-1-4759-9191-8 (hc)
ISBN: 978-1-4759-9190-1 (ebk)

Library of Congress Control Number: 2013909826

Printed in the United States of America

iUniverse rev. date: 05/28/2013

Table of Contents

If you have been sent this book as a gift it's because the sender cares for you and your family. They have sent it because humanity is in danger and the people must awaken to the realities of our world. Please respect them by reading it—what you do afterwards is up to you.

Acknowledgements

I would like to thank everyone who purchased my first book and provided me with the encouragement to produce a second—I hope this meets with as much approval.

It would be impossible for me to do what I do without the love and full support of my wife and family—I love them with all my heart and appreciate them beyond measure.

"I want so much to open your eyes . . .
Tell me that you'll open your eyes"
- Open Your Eyes, Snow Patrol

www.JourneyToABraveNewWorld.com

2. Son of man, speak to the children of thy people, and say unto them, When I bring the sword upon a land, if the people of the land take a man of their coasts, and set him for their watchmen:

3. If when he seeth the sword come upon the land, he blow the trumpet, and warn the people;

4. Then whosoever heareth the sound of the trumpet, and taketh not warning; if the sword come and take him away, his blood shall be upon his own head.

5. He heard the sound of the trumpet, and took not warning; his blood shall be upon him. But he that taketh warning shall deliver his soul.

EZEKIEL 33

THE TRUMPET IS BLOWING

Introduction

In my first book, *Journey to a Brave New World*, I detailed how a small group of satanic worshiping elites are following a multi generational plan to manipulate humanity towards a vision outlined in Aldous Huxley's fictional book *Brave New World*. I detailed how the elites have created and used the concept of Central Banks to consolidate power and steal wealth from the people. I provided evidence showing how this group of Central Bankers, or Banksters, were implicit in starting and extending all the major wars at least since and including World War One. I had provided a brief glimpse into how Communism was set up in Russia and China and how they have been supported by this same group of Bansckters. Specifically I detailed how the Bolshevik Revolution was funded by the Western Bankers, how General Patton was diverted towards the end of World War II so as to allow Stalin to take Berlin. How the Communist were aided with trade during the Korean and Vietnam Wars and how U.S. troops were operationally restricted such to extend the wars.

I exposed their plans for the massive depopulation of our world and how they are covertly sterilizing and soft killing us using vaccines and chemicals such as Bisphenol A which is used in food containers and fluoride which is added to our water, all of which is to help achieve their goals of a global population of around five hundred million people.

I explained many of the tools and scientific techniques they use to control the minds of the masses such that they accept the changes being forced upon them. These include the use of *False Flag* events such as Oklahoma City bombing, London bombing and 9/11. I outlined the use of *Big Brother* technologies that are already here and being used. Finally, I provided some brief details of what we, humanity, can do to change direction.

In this book I will provide further evidence of their intentions for us and especially the United States as they plan our demise. I will outline their plans for using:

-   Civilian internment and labor camps in the United States
-   The use of Communist Troops to complete the takeover of the United States
-   The possible use of a nuclear strike within the United States to take their agenda a step further
-   Second American Civil War

Finally, I will provide a forty five step plan that would enable the United States to regain its former glory and ensure that the satanic worshiping globalist do not get their *Brave New World*.

As with my first book, the golden rule that I ask you to follow is this: if you cannot believe anything that I detail, put the book down, research my claims and only restart once you have confirmed my claims to be true.

The Watchmen are blowing the trumpet—what will you do?

"We cannot continue to rely on our military in order to achieve the national security objectives we've set. We've got to have a civilian national security force that's just as powerful, just as strong, just as well-funded."

—Barack Obama, July 2, 2008

CHAPTER 1

Camps and Orders

Throughout history tyrannical governments have interned their own citizens. Stalin kept 'political dissidents' in Gulags where they were forced into hard labor and ultimately for most, this meant death. Hitler as we all know held Jews in concentration camps where hard labor and gas chambers awaited them. Today, in North Korea, just the suspicion of being a Christian is enough to enslave you and your family with no chance of reprieve.

But this could never happen here in the United States, right? Before we explore current evidence for plans of civilian labor camps inside the United States let's just remind ourselves of what happened during World War II.

On February 19, 1942 Executive Order 9066 was signed by President Franklin D. Roosevelt. This order allowed military commanders to designate certain zones at their discretion as "military areas" for which all people were excluded. Spawning from this Executive Order were several "Civilian Exclusion Orders" culminating in Order number 34 going into effect on May 3, 1942 which ordered all people of Japanese ancestry, whether US citizens or not, to be moved to permanent "Relocation

Centers". Families were given less than forty eight hours notice to report to a Civil Control Station. Only essential personal effects, bedding, basic clothing and basic eating utensils were allowed. No pets or other personal items were permitted. Records indicate that approximately sixty two per cent of the people that were interned were American citizens. They were not formerly charged and they were not allowed a trial. Where was the Constitution for them?

Now let's take a look at some Executive Orders that have been signed in over the last fifty years.

EXECUTIVE ORDER 10990

Allows the government to take over all modes of transport and control of highways and seaports.

EXECUTIVE ORDER 10995

Allows the government to seize and control the communications media

EXECUTIVE ORDER 10997

Allows the government to take over all electrical power, gas, petroleum, fuels and minerals

EXECUTIVE ORDER 10998

Allows the government to take over all food resources and farms

EXECUTIVE ORDER 10999

Assigns emergency preparedness functions to the secretary of commerce.

EXECUTIVE ORDER 11000

Allows the government to take mobilize civilians into work brigades under government supervision.

EXECUTIVE ORDER 11001

Allows the government to take over all health, education and welfare functions.

EXECUTIVE ORDER 11002 designates the Postmaster General to operate a national registration of all persons.

EXECUTIVE ORDER 11003

Allows the government to take over all airports and aircraft, including commercial aircraft.

EXECUTIVE ORDER 11004

Allows the Housing and Finance Authority to relocate communities, build new housing with public funds, designate areas to be abandoned, and establish new locations for populations.

EXECUTIVE ORDER 11005

Allows the government to take over railroads, inland waterways and public storage facilities.

EXECUTIVE ORDER 11049

Assigns emergency preparedness function to federal departments and agencies, consolidating 21 operative Executive Orders issued over a fifteen year period.

EXECUTIVE ORDER 11921

Allows the Federal Emergency Preparedness Agency to develop plans to establish control over the mechanisms of production and distribution, of energy sources, wages, salaries, credit and the flow of money in U.S. financial institution in any undefined national emergency. It also provides that when a state of emergency is declared by the President, Congress cannot review the action for six months.

Important note: These Executive Orders (EO) represent the foundations upon which other Executive Orders have been issued, therefore effectively replacing them. This is a very typical ploy using bait and switch tactics and a spider's web of Executive Orders that is designed to confuse people. This also allows 'them' to counter any "conspiracy theorist" by stating that these Executive Orders are not valid. This is true, they've all been superseded, but the important fact to understand is that the foundations laid still remain intact. By way of example let's look at Executive Order 10998 (ability for government to take over all food resources and farms). EO 10998 was revoked by EO 11490, which was amended by EO's 11522, 11556, 11746, 11921, 11953, 12038, 12046, 12107, 12148, 12608—and then Revoked by EO 12656. EO 11522 was amended by EO 11490 and superseded by EO 11921 which in turn was amended by EO 11556—do you get the picture?

No wonder our representatives don't appeal these—they have no idea of the real intent and of course that's the point.

In addition to the web of Executive Orders we also have Presidential Directives. On May 9th 2007 the Bush Administration issued notice of National Security Presidential Directive 51, Homeland Security Presidential Security Directive HSPD20. In the Presidential Directive it claims power to execute procedures for continuity of the federal government in the event of a "catastrophic emergency". Such an emergency is construed as "any incident, regardless of location, that results in extraordinary levels of mass casualties, damage, or disruption severely affecting the U.S. population, infrastructure, environment, economy, or government functions."

What does this really mean? Basically given the right event it allows Congress and the Senate (and of course the Constitution) to be suspended and replaced by Continuity Of Government (C.O.G.) plans to take over. And what exactly do we know about C.O.G.? Well here's what Prof. Peter Dale Scott reported in Global Research on May 19, 2010.

"In August 2007, Congressman Peter DeFazio, a member of the House Homeland Security Committee, told the House that he and the rest of his Committee had been barred from reviewing parts of National

Security Presidential Directive 51, the White House super secret plans to implement so-called "Continuity of Government" in the event of a mass terror attack or natural disaster."

As I've detailed in my first book, both the Republicans and Democrats are controlled by the same *Shadow Government*, who in turn are funded and controlled by the *Central Bankers* and of course the satanic worshiping 'elites'. To further prove that point here's another Executive Order, this time signed by President Obama on March 16, 2012

Executive Order 13603—National Defense Resources Preparedness

This order includes:

(a) identify requirements for the full spectrum of emergencies, including essential military and civilian demand;
(b) assess on an ongoing basis the capability of the domestic industrial and technological base to satisfy requirements in peacetime and times of national emergency, specifically evaluating the availability of the most critical resource and production sources, including subcontractors and suppliers, materials, skilled labor, and professional and technical personnel;
(c) be prepared, in the event of a potential threat to the security of the United States, to take actions necessary to ensure the availability of adequate resources and production capability, including services and critical technology, for national defense requirements;

This Order uses the term "in peacetime and in times of national emergency" and allows our government to take over control of anything it likes.

Essentially, if the office of the Presidency didn't already have the power to bypass Congress and the Constitution, then they do now.

One problem they had to solve was how to identify who and what they can loot once these *Orders* are in place. And of course this is why they issued a forty six page Census to all farmers insisting that they comply or expect a visit from your friendly government agent.

The Census requires the farmers to detail everything from acreage of land, number and type of livestock held including value, types and yield of crops grown and sources of power used on the farm.

Any self respecting and intelligent thief would first check out their target by spending time watching activities, keeping an eye out for patterns and value of goods and then devising a plan to get in and get out without getting caught. Our government uses the more direct and obvious approach. 'Tell us exactly what you have so we can come by when we want and collect it and please also provide your acceptance for working in our labor camps for sixteen hours a day with no pay. No pressure, but if you don't tell us you'll be put on the Red List.' (see end of this chapter)

So to summarize, the President has the legal means by which he, or the Shadow Government (which Congress is not allowed to know about) can remove our Rights as citizens of the United States, ignore or suspend the Constitution, take away all our belongings and means of sustaining life and force citizens into labor camps. All that is needed is a good excuse.

The plans for these Labor Camps have been in the works for many years, but only came to light during the 1987 Iran-Contra hearings. At this hearing Congressman Brooks questioned Lieutenant Colonel Oliver North about his role in continuity of government plans. He was politely told by Senator Inouye that this was "a highly sensitive and classified area" and requested that questions not be asked. Congressman Brooks continued and asked about contingency plans that included suspending the Constitution. Although he was again shut down it did alert people to these behind the scene plans.

It was later discovered that during 1984 the U.S. Armed Forces conducted a national exercise named Readiness Exercise 84, or nor more commonly referred to as REX 84. REX 84 was designed as a test of the military's ability to detain large numbers of American citizens during civil unrest or a national emergency. Further research uncovered that plans were in place to allow FEMA to take control of Federal and State governments, the military would take the place of elected leaders and the plan called for rounding up twenty one million "American Negroes" and place them in FEMA relocation camps.

It was later discovered that REX 84 was a subset of a much larger plan titled "Department of Defense Civil Disturbance Plan 55-2" using the code name Operation Garden Plot. Operation Garden Plot was created to allow for the establishment of a nationwide state of martial law to be declared.

Still not convinced? Let's now look at official Army manuals and documents that further prove they are just ready and waiting, possibly for you.

FM 3-39.40 Internment and Resettlement Operations, Department of the Army, February 2010

This Army manual defines the procedures to be followed for the internment and resettlement (I/R) of detainees which includes U.S. Military prisoners and dislocated civilians.

A dislocated civilian is defined as follows:

> "The term *dislocated civilian* is a broad term that includes a displaced person, an evacuee, an expellee, an internally displaced person, a migrant, a refugee, or a stateless person"

They further define these categories:

Evacuee: "An *evacuee* is a civilian removed from a place of residence by military direction for reasons of personal security or the requirements of the military situation"

Internally displaced person: "An *internally displaced person* is any person who has left their residence by reason of real or imagined danger but has not left the territory of their own country. Internally displaced persons may have been forced to flee their homes for the same reasons as refugees, but have not crossed an internationally recognized border."

It also states that if your status cannot be determined you are to be treated as an EPW—Enemy Prisoner of War.

The manual describes the role and functions of the Psychological Operations Officer which includes:

> "Develops PSYOP products that are designed to pacify and acclimate detainees or DCs to accept U.S. I/R [Internment / Resettlement] facility authority and regulations."

If you're thinking that while in these camps you might get bored, don't worry, they have plenty of 'educational' opportunities. And if you don't behave according to regulations, no problem, there's a reeducation program to help you improve.

> "K-24. The audiovisual team can support three or more tactical PSYOP detachments when supporting I/R operations. The audiovisual team uses organic equipment to produce and disseminate products to the I/R facility population. The team supports the facility PSYOP program by disseminating entertainment products, such as videos and music. This team gives the tactical PSYOP detachment the ability to influence detainee and DC behavior by providing or withholding something of value to the population. When directed, the team disseminates products that support other PSYOP task force programs (reeducation, reorientation, posthostility themes)." {sic}

Another interesting read is Army Field Manual FM 3-19.15 Civil Disturbance Operations. This two hundred and fifty page manual describes the tactics the Army can use to control civil disturbances.

Not only does it deal with disturbance on the streets, but also disturbance in "Confinement Facilities". This ties in nicely with Internment and Resettlement camps detailed previously. One option open to them is the use of chemicals.

> "The use of chemical irritants can be a valuable NL tool for control force leadership to consider during the planning phase.

These chemical irritants can drive a threat from an established, enclosed position or deny the rioters access to a certain area without long-lasting effects to those involved. The proper use of chemical irritants may prevent the control force from having to enter a dangerous area; however, improper use can cause injury, death, or property damage."

Carrying on with this theme let's review another U.S. Army Manual—Army regulation 210-35, Civilian Inmate Labor Program.

In the summary of this document issued in 2005 it states:

"This regulation provides guidance for establishing and managing civilian inmate labor programs on Army installations. It provides guidance on establishing prison camps on Army installations. It addresses record keeping and reporting incidents related to Civilian Inmate Labor Program and/or prison camp administration."

It explains how it benefits the army by:

"Providing a source of labor at no direct labor cost to Army installations to accomplish tasks that would not be possible otherwise due to the manning and funding constraints under which the Army operates."

It further clarifies that:

"Inmates are not Department of the Army employees and are not regarded as such. Inmates must not be referred to as employees. They will not be paid from Department of the Army funds, nor receive any personal or private gratuity for work accomplished or services rendered."

And

"The Civilian Inmate Labor Program was created to provide installation commanders with an alternate labor source to perform valid requirements. Civilian inmate labor does not compete with existing in-house or contractor resources."

It's also interesting to note that the U.S. Army is currently recruiting for "Internment/Resettlement Specialist (31E)" and details the job as:

"Internment/resettlement specialists are primarily responsible for day-to-day operations in a military confinement/correctional facility or detention/internment facility."

So we have detailed the existence of plans to round up and detain civilians, use them for free labor and even to reeducate them if they misbehave, but how will they convince the people to go quietly into these camps?

Romans Chapter 13

August 23, 2007 KSLA news in Shreveport Louisiana reported the following:

"Could martial law ever become a reality in America? Some fear any nuclear, biological or chemical attack on U.S. soil might trigger just that. KSLA News 12 has discovered that the clergy would help the government with potentially their biggest problem: Us."

They reported how guns were being confiscated in the aftermath of hurricane Katrina and the elimination of the Posse Comitatus act of 1878 (which was eliminated after the False Flag event—9/11)

They continued to report that:

"If martial law were enacted here at home, like depicted in the movie "The Siege", easing public fears and quelling dissent would be critical. And that's exactly what the 'Clergy Response Team' helped accomplish in the wake of Katrina . . . .

> For the clergy team, one of the biggest tools that they will have
> in helping calm the public down or to obey the law is the bible
> itself, specifically Romans 13."

In a report on Infowars.com on December 19, 2011 it details that in May of 2011 the government website FedBizOps.gov posted a Department of Homeland Security solicitation titled "National Responder Support Camp", Solicitation Number: HSFEHQ-10-R-0027, which requested contractors to construct and operate Responder Support Camps. In the article written by Kurt Nimmo he states:

> ""responder camps" are less about coordinating response to
> hurricanes than assisting in the implementation and facilitation
> of a police state apparatus during martial law and establishment
> political events covered under NSSE (National Special Security
> Events)."

In another Infowars.com article this time related to the National Defense Authorization Act (NDAA), dated December 12, 2011, Paul Joseph Watson details how Obama had stated that he would veto the Bill and yet Senator Carl Levin has gone on record saying that Obama was actually lobbying for the removal of the language that would have protected American citizens from being detained indefinitely and without trial. The NDAA was signed by President Obama just before midnight on December 31st 2011. Presidential candidate Ron Paul stated that "The NDAA Bill begins the official establishment of martial law in the United States."

He went on to say,

"This step where they can literally arrest American people, American citizens and put them away without a trial, and you heard Lindsey Graham say 'well if they ask for a lawyer, tell them no lawyer for you.' I mean that is arrogant and bold and dangerous."

In one episode of former Governor Jesse Ventura's "Conspiracy Theory" television show which aired once on TruTv, he addresses the "conspiracy" of the secret government plan to round up and imprison Americans in concentration camps. The show exposes the FUSION centers that are used as Command Centers to 'collect' and share intelligence data on American citizens. They also expose the storage facilities containing hundreds of thousands of multi body plastic coffins—See chapter 4, Civil War Two and an American Genocide?

As mentioned, this episode was only shown once. It was not repeated, unlike the shows other episodes. At present the full episode can be watched at :

http://www.thenewalexandrialibrary.com/policestate.html

Now that we have established the fact that the civilian labor camps and detention camps are real and for U.S. Citizens, and that the laws and procedures are in place and ready for action let's now consider the following question:

Will U.S. Troops fire on U.S. Civilians if ordered to do so?

Unfortunately this is a serious question and one that was reportedly posed to soldiers returning from duty in 1994. A U.S. Armed Services Survey was given to select servicemen in which the following question was posed:

46: The U.S. government declares a ban on the possession, sale, transportation, and transfer of all non-sporting firearms. A thirty (30) day amnesty period is permitted for these firearms to be turned over to the local authorities. At the end of this period, a number of citizen groups refuse to turn over their firearms. Consider the following statement: I would fire on U.S. citizens who refuse or resist confiscation of firearms banned by the U.S. government?

Strongly agree (___)
Agree (___)
Disagree (___)
Strongly Disagree (___)
No opinion (___)

Other questions that were asked included:

"Are we to turn over our armed forces to the U.N.?"

"Should we compromise our U.S. Constitution in the name of world government?"

"Do you believe in a New World Order run by the United Nations?"

And the results or the survey?

"About one in four U.S. Marines would be willing to fire upon American citizens in a government gun confiscation program, according to the results of a survey undertaken nearly a year ago at a Marine Corps Base in Southern California . . . . 18.67 percent or 56 Marines, indicated they "agree" with the statement, and 7.67 percent or 23 Marines, indicated that "strongly agree." The Spotlight, April 25, 1995, Mike Blair

For me this is very disturbing, but on the positive side at least the majority disagreed. Perhaps this is the reason why foreign troops have been training in the U.S. for several years (see Chapter 3), but before we explore that let's look at a recent Facebook blog made by Noble Peace Prize nominee, Jim Garrow, who claims he was told by a top military veteran that the Obama administration's new "litmus test" for new military leaders is whether or not they would obey an order to fire on U.S. Citizens. He went on to state that those who said "no" would be removed.

It is my contention that hurricane Katrina was used as a trial balloon to test the acceptance of the people to give up their guns and other belongings and be shepherded into the makeshift shelters and camps. I do not believe that it was simply incompetence that delayed supplies of food and fresh water by about four days. Hopefully, this incident triggered many people to take responsibility for their own disaster preparations, but don't worry the government has contingency plans for those people too.

Examiner.com, August 11, 2011—FBI adds 'preppers' to potential terrorist list.

> "An FBI Denver Joint Terrorism Task Force handout being distributed to Colorado military surplus store owners lists the purchase of popular preparedness items and firearms accessories as 'suspicious' and 'potential indicators of terrorist activities,'"

Catch 22? Yes, that's right, if you don't prepare to look after yourself following a major event or disaster you can expect to be welcomed into one of the many Civilian Inmate Labor camps, however if you do prepare, watch out, you could be considered a terrorist and therefore under provisions detailed in the NDAA you could be arrested and interned indefinitely and without trial.

Are you still wondering why our government wants you disarmed?

Actually, if we are to agree that "preppers" are potential terrorists, then I guess our government must be considered the biggest terrorist of all, especially given the amount of ammo and preparations they have been taking over the last few years.

✱ ✱ ✱

Over the last decade there have many urban training drills run by the military on U.S. soil which enable troops to practice going door to door for gun confiscation or rounding up potential domestic terrorists. One such drill that I will detail here is the "Urban Warfare Drill" held in Arcadia, Iowa in April 2009.

Speaking on the Alex Jones radio show, Lt. Colonel Greg Hapgood spoke about how they were training soldiers in the art of "cordon and search". They would cordon off an area such that no-one could enter or leave and then search for weapons, person of interest or other contraband.

I've detailed before in my first book how television shows and movies are used to prepare the population for what is to come by the use of *predictive programming*. Now just think of all the shows and movies that depict U.S. troops operating inside the United States. It might surprise you when you realize just how many there are. It should not be forgotten that the Posse Comitatus act of 1878 was designed to ensure that tyrants couldn't take over the U.S. using military force—but of course since the false flag 9/11 event, this has been ignored.

Before we close on this chapter let's look at what Officer Jack McLamb (retired), probably the most highly decorated officer in the Phoenix Police Department, while addressing a group on the steps of the White House said:

> "I want to tell you about the red and blue lists . . . . I've had people calling me saying they go out to their mailbox and they find a little red dot or a little blue dot on their mailbox, and they wonder what the little red dot and blue dot is. Well it's marking your mailboxes by the government so that when foreign troops come in after martial law, if you have a red dot they take you out immediately and shoot you right there in the head, but if you have a blue dot they take you to the FEMA camps being built by Haliburton right now."

"Brownie, you're doing a heck of a job."

—President G.W. Bush
to FEMA Director Michael Brown
in the aftermath and debacle of Hurricane Katrina.

CHAPTER 2

It's a Regional Problem

If you are on the *Blue List* it might be worth taking a couple of seconds out of your day to think about which camp you'd like to be dragged away to. Just as a reminder, each family member will need to make their own choice too. In an article by David Hodge on thecommonsenseshow.com he states:

> "Your family will subsequently be separated by the authorities as a prelude to sending you to a FEMA camp, and that means that men will go to one facility, and women will go to another. Children will have their own facility awaiting them. In all likelihood, this will mark the last time you will ever see your family. How do I know this? Read the Rex 84 documents."

With literally hundreds to choose from it can be a hard choice. Many websites suggests that there are over eight hundred locations around the United States that are either immediately ready to welcome *guests* or could be very quickly adapted to do so. You can research the list of locations by using:

INTERNET SEARCH TERM: 800 FEMA CAMPS

I know, just because it's on the *web* it doesn't mean it's real. So with that in mind let's look at:

H.R. 390 National Emergency Centers Establishment Act—January 23, 2013

From Section two of the Bill:

> "In General—In accordance with the requirements of this Act, the Secretary of Homeland Security shall establish not fewer than 6 national emergency centers on military installations.
>
> (b) Purpose of National Emergency Centers—The purpose of a national emergency center shall be to use existing infrastructure—
>
> (1) to provide temporary housing, medical, and humanitarian assistance to individuals and families dislocated due to an emergency or major disaster;
>
> (2) to provide centralized locations for the purposes of training and ensuring the coordination of Federal, State, and local first responders"

Section three is titled "DESIGNATION OF MILITARY INSTALLATIONS AS NATIONAL EMERGENCY CENTERS."

If you can't decide on a particular location how about selecting your preferred region. From the same H.R. 390 act we discover the following:

> "Location of National Emergency Centers—There shall be established not fewer than one national emergency center in each of the following areas:
>
> (1) The area consisting of Federal Emergency Management Agency Regions I, II, and III.

(2) The area consisting of Federal Emergency Management Agency Region IV.

(3) The area consisting of Federal Emergency Management Agency Regions V and VII.

(4) The area consisting of Federal Emergency Management Agency Region VI.

(5) The area consisting of Federal Emergency Management Agency Regions VIII and X.

(6) The area consisting of Federal Emergency Management Agency Region IX."

FEMA has designated ten regions within the United States. You can verify this at www.fema.gov, but to save you some time, here they are:

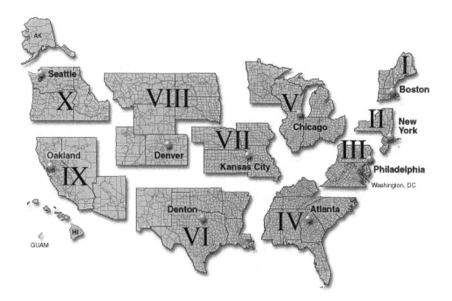

Just who will be responsible for running these ten regions? Canada Free Press printed the following on January 12, 2010

"American Republic Replaced by 'Council of Governors'"

In this they state that:

> "Quietly—even stealthily—in the opening days of the New Year, President Barack Obama has set up a "Council of Governors"."

The article continues to detail the Executive Order titled Establishment of the Council of Governors:

> "Obama signed an executive order establishing a panel to be known as the Council of Governors, which will be made up of 10 state governors, to be selected by the president to serve two-year terms. Members will review matters involving the National Guard; homeland defense; civil support; and synchronization and integration of state and federal military activities in the United States, the White House said in a statement."

In September 2009 one of these FEMA detention centers in FEMA Region VIII near Hardin, Montana was exposed by Steve Quayle and Alex Jones. The Two Rivers FEMA camp was policed by a group called "American Police Force". This *American Police Force* used black Mercedes SUV's which claimed that they were a part of Hardin Police, even though Hardin didn't have its own Police department and which included the logo of a two headed eagle or phoenix, exactly the same as is used on the Serbian coat of arms. The Mayor of Hardin at the time, Ron Adams denied that they were part of the official Hardin Police.

Further research uncovered the fact that this facility could handle at least ten thousand detainees and that it was being manned by foreigners.

Are the pieces of the puzzle now fitting together?

"The individual is handicapped by coming face-to-face with a conspiracy so monstrous he cannot believe it exists."

—J. Edgar Hoover

"Today Americans would be outraged if U.N. troops entered Los Angeles to restore order; tomorrow they will be grateful,"

—Henry Kissinger, 1991

CHAPTER 3

Foreign Troops

In the 1984 movie classic "Red Dawn" we are presented with a scenario whereby Soviet, Nicaraguan and Cuban troops are seen parachuting onto a high school field in Colorado and start shooting people on sight. Those that were not immediately killed were rounded up and placed into internment camps. A small group of mostly teenagers did manage to escape and hid in the mountains where they later formed a guerilla force named the "Wolverines". The follow up to this movie Red Dawn 2 released in 2012 is essentially a remake, however this time the U.S. is invaded by North Korean troops. Interestingly, this movie was to be released in 2010 and was to depict a Chinese army invading the U.S. In the movie we learn that Korea and China capture the West coast while Russian troops capture the East coast.

In this chapter we will look at reports of foreign troops training on U.S. soil and discuss the possibility of Russian and Chinese troops being used as a tool to complete the takedown of the United States. This is something I briefly discussed in my first book.

Alex Jones, the host of Infowars Radio show was one of the first to uncover and report on the use of foreign troop in the late 1990's when he reported on Operation Urban Warrior in a documentary titled "POLICE STATE 2000." In this documentary we see Marines practicing for gun confiscation and setting up concentration camps working alongside foreign troops including Chinese and Russians.

On April 20, 2012 a Chinese news agency in Xinhua reported that Russian and U.S. troops were to conduct anti terror drills between May 24 and 31, 2012 in Colorado. A Russian spokesman, Alexander Kucherenko said:

> "According to the exercise scenario, soldiers of the two countries will hold tactical airborne operation, including the reconnaissance of an imaginary terrorists' camp and a raid"

He went on to explain that Russian forces will use U.S. Special Service Weapons at drills in Fort Carson, Colorado.

On April 24 2012 the EUTimes reported the following:

US Calls For Russian Airborne Troops To Take And Hold Denver Airport

> "A bizarre report prepared by the Federal Service for Military-Technical Cooperation that is circulating in the Kremlin today on the joint US-Russia military drills taking place next month in the State of Colorado says that the plans received from the Americans call for Russian Airborne Troops during this strange exercise to "take and hold" the Central Intelligence Agencies (CIA) main facility, the National Security Agencies (NSA) main facility and the Denver International Airport (DIA)."

The article continues to explain that Russian airborne troops will be using US weapons that they had previously trained with at Fort Carson. The objective of the exercise was to parachute from their planes, seize the CIA's main computer facility in Denver, the NSA's main computer facility in Bluffdale, UT and taking control of main runways and terminals of the Denver International Airport.

Another multi national exercise, this time with U.S., Russian and Canadian forces, called Vigilant Eagle 12 was conducted at Peterson Air Force Base in Colorado as reported in NORAD News. It details how the exercise was to focus on hijacked aircraft as they move from Russian to U.S. airspace.

Business Insider news reported on another similar exercise called Operation Attentive Eagle 2012 which had Russian forces training inside NORAD. They reported:

> "It might not be the best idea to invite Washington's nearest nuclear competitor to an installation designed to repel a nuclear war. Then again, the Cold War is over. Operation Attentive Eagle 2012 ended today after three days at NORAD, the U.S.-Canadian jointly operated North American Aerospace Defense Command."

In addition to these training exercises the United States has signed an agreement with Canada to allow for military forces to be used across border during an emergency.

Ottawa Citizen, February 22, 2008—Canada, U.S. quietly sign military aid pact.

> "Canada and the U.S. have signed an agreement that paves the way for the militaries from either nation to send troops across each other's borders during an emergency, but some are questioning why the Harper government has kept silent on the deal.
>
> Neither the Canadian government nor the Canadian Forces announced the new agreement, which was signed Feb. 14 in Texas.

The U.S. military's Northern Command, however, publicized the agreement with a statement outlining how its top officer, Gen. Gene Renuart, and Canadian Lt.-Gen. Marc Dumais, head of Canada Command, signed the plan, which allows the military from one nation to support the armed forces of the other nation during a civil emergency."

Perhaps now you can begin to understand why I believe we will see foreign troops, most likely Russians, following a major event within the United States. What form could that major event possibly take?

Read on.

"Those weapons of mass destruction have got to be here somewhere . . . . No, no weapons over there, maybe under here?"

—George W. Bush, March 2004

CHAPTER 4

Missing for Action? Nukes

When George W. Bush stood before hundreds of journalists and media people at a dinner event in March 2004 and laughed about the inability of coalition forces to find any weapons of mass destruction the entire audience laughed loudly along with him. The next day of course the White House Press Secretary and the Public Relations team had some extra work on their hands as it sunk in that our President had just made a joke about the fact that millions of people died purely on the basis that Iraq had WMD's and were about to use them.

According to The Guardian News Company the total number of nuclear weapons in World in 2009 was 23,574, which is 8,938 less than the total number reported in 2000. Of course this assumes that you believe that Russia disposed of 8,013 since their count went from 21,000 warheads in 2000 to 12,987 in 2009. I for one do not believe that at all and I'll explain why later.

Immediately after the false flag event known as 9/11, we started hearing how easy it would be for radical Muslims to sneak across the border and detonate one of the hundreds of suitcase nukes that Osama Bin Laden was reported to have purchased from high ranking Russians. Here's just one example of such a report:

New York Daily News, November 10, 2001—I Have Nukes Set To Strike U.S.—Osama

The article includes:

> ". . . President Bush warned that Bin Laden's shadowy Al Qaeda terror network was out to get nuclear weapons—and might already have them."

The mainstream media around the World continued with the hype as BBC on March 7, 2002 reported "Fears over missing nuclear material" in which it reported that the World may be awash with weapons grade stolen material.

Of course, now we know the truth about 9/11, we know that these reports were required to keep the public in fear and ensure that we don't rebel against the assault on our freedoms. But, when it's revealed that nuclear weapons go missing from the U.S. Military that news barely sees the light of day. To help answer why that might be let's remind ourselves of something I covered in my first book.

I had previously detailed how the satanic worshiping "elite" bloodlines just love to play their games and regularly give clues as to what they are planning through the use of television shows, movies and books. I provided two specific examples of a television show, Jericho, and a "slide show story" printed in the Telegraph both of which were based on nuclear weapons being detonated in several cities across the United States. At the end of the stories we discover that these nukes were deliberately exploded by elements within our own government. This is a theme that was echoed in one of the series of "24", a hugely popular TV show starring Kiefer Sutherland. I also explained how a coded message reading "this is not simply entertainment" was embedded into the Telegraphs slide show story. This is known as Predictive Programming and is used to manipulate the minds of the people.

Back to those missing nukes, well I'll get there soon, I promise.

In mid to late August 2007 several web sites, including Reuters and blogs were posting news of an extraordinary bet being made in the stock market. Canada Free Press reported the following:

MASSIVE WALL STREET PUT OPTIONS SIGNAL UPCOMING TERROR ATTACK—September 4, 2007

"$4.5 billion options bet on catastrophe within four weeks"

The article details how PUT options, similar to what happened just prior to 9/11, were made that would result in a $4.5 Billion windfall if the S&P 700 value would fall by more than fifty per cent with four weeks.

Here's what they reported:

> "The entity or individual offering these sales can only make money if the market drops 30%-50% within the next four weeks. If the market does not drop, the entity or individual involved stands to lose over $1 billion just for engaging in these contracts! Clearly, someone knows something big is going to happen BEFORE the options expire on Sept. 21."

So for all you budding Columbo's, scratch your head, pull out your notepad and write the following. Clue—someone was betting BIG that something major would happen to cause such a drop in the market. Bets were placed on August 21st 2007.

Now, as promised back to those missing nukes.

The 'Patriot Community' was wild with news that six nuclear bombs were 'lost' for thirty six hours during August 29/30, 2007 (just a week after the $4.5 B bet). The Military Times first reported the news after servicemen leaked the story, but it was rapidly disseminated across many patriot groups across the country.

Reports were verified that six W80-1 Nuclear warheads armed on AGM-129 Advanced Cruise Missiles were lost after taking off from U.S.A.F. Base Minot, North Dakota to U.S.A.F Base Barksdale in Louisiana. Global Research provided an in-depth report on the event and included the following:

> "As Robert Stormer, a former U.S. lieutenant-commander in the U.S. Navy, has commented: "Press reports initially cited the Air Force mistake of flying nuclear weapons over the United States in violation of Air Force standing orders and international treaties, while completely missing the more important major issues, such as how six nuclear cruise missiles got loose to begin with.""

The report also suggests:

> "For those who have been observing these series of "unclear" events it is becoming "clear" that a criminal government is at the helm of the United States. There was no way that the six nuclear missiles could have been "mistakenly" loaded, especially when their separate warheads had to be affixed to the missiles by individuals specialized in such a momentous task."

And

> "The fact that the incident only apparently became known to the U.S. Air Force when military personnel reported it, suggests that either the nuclear weapons were ordered to be moved or that the electronic tracking devices had been removed or tampered with. This scenario would need the involvement of individuals with expertise in military electronics or for those responsible for the monitoring of nuclear weapons to look the other way or both."

Is there any chance that the truth of what really happened will ever be exposed? I suggest it's very unlikely especially given the number of 'mysterious' deaths that occurred with people associated with the incident. Here's a few details.

Airman 1st Class Todd Blue, Died September 10, 2007 he was stationed at Minot U.S.A.F. Base the 5th Security Forces Squadron and was responsible for base entry requirements and a particular section, the Weapons System Security section.

U.S. Air Force Captain John Frueh, found dead September 8, 2007. He was reported as being last seen with a GPS device, camera, and camcorder being carried with him in a backpack. Local police in Oregon and the F.B.I. seemed to be looking for him for days. His family also felt that something bad had happened to him. His role included missions related to conduct of global special operations. These operations—and this is where careful attention should be paid—range from "precision application of firepower, such as nuclear weapons,"

Senior Airman Clint Huff, Died September 15, 2007. He and his wife died in a motorcycle accident near U.S.A.F. Base Barksdale.

Three other Minot based airmen also died in the month before the nukes went missing and it should be noted that an Air Force official, Charles D. Riechers (October 14, 2007) & retired General Russell Elliot Dougherty (September 7, 2007) both had links to the missing nukes and both reportedly committed suicide.

Global Research also points out that several officers were appointed to new Command positions in June 2007 and that George W. Bush met with senior officers from U.S.A.F. Base Minot on June 15, 2007.

Now just what would Columbo make of all this? I'll let you make up your own mind on this one.

Is the Minot incident the only 'mistake' made by our military relating to nuclear weapons? Apparently not.

NBC News.com, March 27, 2008—Gates Orders Full Nuclear Weapons Inventory.

> "Defense Secretary Robert Gates has ordered a full inventory of all nuclear weapons and related materials after the mistaken delivery of ballistic missile fuses to Taiwan, the Pentagon said Thursday."

> "Earlier this week, Gates directed Navy Adm. Kirkland H. Donald to take charge of a full investigation of the delivery mistake in which four cone-shaped electrical fuses used in intercontinental ballistic missile warheads were shipped to the Taiwanese instead of the helicopter batteries they had ordered."

Whatever your thoughts, one thing is clear. The mainstream media is continuing to push the "missing nuclear materials" story.

ABC news, Feb 16, 2005—Official: Enough Material Missing From Russia to Build a Nuke.

In this article they detail that the then Director of the CIA, Porter Goss warned:

> "Goss said he could not assure the American people that the missing nuclear material had not found its way into terrorists' hands."

Bloomberg, March 26,2012—Missing Nukes Fuel Terror Concern as Obama Drawn to Seoul.

This article explains that fifty countries participated in the second global conference concerning the escape of nuclear material from state control.

> "The legacy of the Soviet Union's breakup, inadequate atomic stockpile controls and the proliferation of nuclear-fuel technology mean the world may be awash with unaccounted-for weapons ingredients, ripe to be picked up by terrorists."

Just a quick note here. Do you notice how the 2012 Bloomberg article and the 2002 BBC article (earlier in this chapter) both use the phrase "World may be awash". Having studied their propaganda tricks for several years, I can tell you that this looks like they are following the same given script.

Mumbai, Daily News & Analysis, June 19, 2012—The big threat: Nuclear material continues to go missing in India

> "A joint study conducted by British and Indian experts suggest there is clear danger from chemical, biological and radiological (CBR) materials falling into wrong hands within India's borders.
>
> While releasing the report prepared jointly by the Royal United Services Institute (RUSI) and the Delhi-based Observer Research Foundation (ORF), former Union home secretary GK Pillai said the government woke up to CBR threats after discovering disappearance of 14,000 tonnes of chemicals in Madhya Pradesh three years ago."

They only woke up to the threat after 14,000 tons of chemicals go missing? How on earth does 14,000 tons go missing? A large capacity tanker truck carries about 9,000 gallons which is roughly equivalent to 283 tons, therefore 14,000 tons would represent about forty nine fully loaded large capacity trucks. Here's where I scratch my head and get my notebook out—I just need to find a pen . . .

When the Council on Foreign Relations (CFR), an off shoot of the Royal Institute of International Affairs and effectively the U.S. 'Shadow government' makes a statement about missing nukes you better pay careful attention. In January 2006 they issued a paper titled "Loose Nukes" in which they provide the following:

> "Have terrorist organizations ever tried to obtain nuclear weapons?—
>
> Yes. Russian authorities say that in the past three years alone they have broken up hundreds of nuclear-material smuggling

deals. In October 2001, shortly after the World Trade Center attacks, a Russian nuclear official reported having foiled two separate incidents over the previous eight months in which terrorists had "staked out" a secret weapons storage site. In the 1990s, U.S. authorities discovered several al-Qaeda plots to obtain nuclear materials, and former CIA Director George Tenet told the Senate Select Committee on Intelligence that Osama bin Laden had sought to "acquire or develop a nuclear device."

* * *

At this point I think we should consider a statement I made in my first book

> "Communist Take Over—Russia and China were set up, encouraged and helped by the Western Ruling class (the New World Order) for one reason—Russian and Chinese troops will be used to complete the takeover of the United States."

When Karl Marx and Friedrich Engels wrote the Communist Manifesto in the mid 1800's they made it very clear that their objective was to "dethrone God and destroy capitalism". If you think that the tearing down of the Berlin Wall and the end of the Cold War was the end of the Communist threat, think again. A One World Socialist Government is the stated aim of the Globalist ruling elites. This move was simply another bait and switch. Joel M. Skousen provides an excellent overview of the "phony collapse of the Soviet Union" in his book "Strategic Relocation—3rd Edition", which was published in 2010. He also states:

> "They intend, we believe, to launch a massive nuclear surprise attack, without warning upon US and English military targets—after an appropriate trigger event (probably in Korea or Taiwan)."

This statement aligns with claims made by Russia's highest ranking military defector, Stanislav Lunev.

In his book "Through the Eyes of the Enemy" he states:

> "Though most Americans don't realize it, America is already penetrated by Russian military special forces—or *Spetznatz* . . . . These elite special forces are under the control of my former employer, the GRU. Some units are assigned to the Special Destinations Group. They penetrate countries shortly before a war and perform military sabotage that Americans would call terrorism . . . . During wartime, they would try to assassinate as many American leaders as possible, as well as their families . . . . One of the GRU's major tasks is to find drop sites for their supplies of clothes, cash, and special equipment—including even small nuclear devices, the so called 'suitcase bombs' . . . . When the nuclear bomb is to be activated, *Spetznatz* soldiers will retrieve it and take it to a safe area for initial preparation. Should the final order be given to explode the weapon, they will take it to the target, set the timer, and leave . . . . Russia has also been a leader in the development of 'Electromagnetic Pulse' weapons. Basically, EMP's were identified during early nuclear testing . . . Large scale EMP weapons can cripple cities. Probably the most troubling set of weapons that Russians are pursuing involves the use of very, very low frequency radio signals . . . Russian research indicates that these radio signals—used at nonlethal level and combined with other types of radiation—can be used to put people into a zombie-like state."

Could this be why we are seeing so many zombie movies and DHS/CDC drills based on 'zombie attacks'?

Before we move onto the next topic let's take a summation of the last three chapters. I have detailed the National Defense Authorization Act (NDAA), Presidential Directive 51 (PD51) and the many Executive Orders that allow the President to enact Martial Law, suspend the Constitution and detain Americans without charge or trial. I've detailed the readiness of large scale Civilian internment & labor camps. I have provided evidence of foreign troops, especially Russian, who are conducting training exercises using American weapons within the United States and I have outlined several reasons why we should be weary of either a nuclear false flag attack or possibly a massive Russian attack.

Am I the only person concerned that something very big is going to happen soon? Let's move to the next chapter and see.

"Just as the sun worship of the Aztecs demanded the painful death of thousands of human beings annually, so the new scientific religion will demand its holocausts of sacred victims."

-Lord Bertrand Russell, "The Scientific Outlook" 1931

"The nine most terrifying words in the English language are: I'm from the government and I'm here to help."

—President Reagan Aug. 12, 1986

CHAPTER 5

Civil War Two and an American Genocide?

Previously we touched on an episode from former Governor Jesse Ventura's television show 'Conspiracy Theory' which detailed plans for Civilian internment camps in the United States, the Fusion centers that have been set up to monitor 'domestic terrorists' and the storage facilities containing at least half a million plastic coffins capable of holding at least two adults. At the time of filming the show these coffins were being stored near Madison, Georgia. The manufacturer of these coffins, or vaults, as they call them, show pricing to be $120 per coffin/vault. Whilst I doubt that FEMA paid that much, it still begs the question—why would FEMA see the need to spend about $60 million of tax payer money on these, especially when our country is almost $17 Trillion in debt, unless of course they were expecting to use them.

This is not the only case of planning for mass casualties and mass civilian displacement that has been discovered.

The governments own website FEDBIZOPPS.GOZ (FBO.GOV) has many solicitations listed that prove that something big is expected. Here's a few examples:

Solicitation Number: HSFEHQ-11-R-Meals—Department of Homeland Security, Office FEMA—Jan 20, 2011

This is a solicitation for provision of 14 million meals per day for 7 million survivors following a "catastrophic disaster event within the New Madrid Fault"

Solicitation Number: HSFE70-12-R-0019—Department of Homeland Security, Office FEMA—Sept 18, 2012

This $64 Million contract was awarded for:

> "FEMA is planning to set up an IDIQ (Indefinite Delivery, Indefinite Quantity) contract to procure commercial and reduced-sodium meals for future requirements. All meals must be shelf stable, self-heating, and include an entree along with additional meal components that can be consumed either as part of the meal or reserved for a supplemental snack."

Solicitation Number: HSFE90-12-R-0035—Department of Homeland Security, Office FEMA—Sept 26, 2012

> "The Request for Proposal is for Program Management Support (subject matter experts) for the FEMA Domestic Emergency Support Team and Nuclear Incident Response Team. Place of Performance is Washington DC and Contractor's location."

On September 28, 2012 a Bill titled H.R. 6566 (112th): Mass Fatality Planning and Religious Consideration Act was passed in Congress. The Bill provide for:

> "Preparedness for Mass Fatalities—In carrying out this section, the Administrator shall provide guidance to and coordinate

with appropriate individuals, including representatives from different communities, private sector businesses, non-profit organizations, and religious organizations, to prepare for and respond to a natural disaster, act of terrorism, or other man-made disaster that results in mass fatalities."

On April 4, 2007, the State of New York Division of Cemeteries sent out "Mass Fatality forms" to cemeteries in that state to collect data about their ability to deal with the high volume of casualties that would occur if there were a flu pandemic or other disaster.

The letter stated:

"Much of this data will be very important in the planning for a mass fatality or pandemic situation. You may be hearing of special meetings in your region that will address planning for such events and we encourage you to attend and take part in those meetings."

Included in this survey was:

"Should a prolonged mass fatality disaster or pandemic flu occur in your community would your cemetery be able to provide temporary or permanent internment space for a significant number of disaster or flu deaths in addition to your current burial services?"

Cemetery owners were also asked to detail the business structure and capacity of their facilities, including proximity to roads, train lines and airfields. The Division of Cemeteries requested data to calculate the number of acres that could be made available "at 950 graves per acre."

Between May 16 to 20, 2011 a national exercise took place known as National Level Exercise 11 (NLE 11)—this exercise as detailed in the State of Missouri website, was a five-day training exercise focused on a coordinated local, state and federal response to a magnitude 7.7 New Madrid Seismic Zone (NMSZ) earthquake. The exercise, known as the

National Level Exercise 2011 was designed to prepare and coordinate a multiple-jurisdictional integrated response to a national catastrophic event—specifically a major earthquake in the central United States region NMSZ.

You might argue that since devastating earthquakes have occurred in the New Madrid zone before, being ready for such a natural disaster is simply good preparedness, but what cannot be explained away using a similar argument is why is the Department of Homeland Security building up a massive arsenal of ammo, weapons and armored vehicles?

At the time of writing this book (March 2013) the provable purchases of ammo for the last eighteen months exceeds two billion rounds—equivalent to six bullets per person, regardless of age, living in the United States or equivalent to about twenty eight years worth of ammo based on the fact that the U.S. military fired seventy million rounds in one year of the Iraq War.

The ammo being purchased included many different calibers including .223, .308 (used in sniper rifles) and various caliber "hollow points" which are bullets that expand on contact causing maximum damage. These are bullets you would not use for simple training and target shooting.

Examples of contract being solicited on FEDBIZOPPS.GOV

Solicitation Number: HSFLAR-13-Q-00020

Agency: Department of Homeland Security
Office: Federal Law Enforcement Training Center (FLETC)

Request for 360,000 rounds of pistol .40 caliber 165 grain and jacketed hollow point (JHP)

Solicitation Number: HSCEMS-12-R-00015
Agency: Department of Homeland Security
Office: Immigration & Customs Enforcement

This solicitation is for thirty three million rounds of .223 in the base year and in each year of the four option years—potential total of one hundred and sixty five million rounds.

Solicitation Number: HSFLGL-12-B-00003
Agency: Department of Homeland Security
Office: Federal Law Enforcement Trng Ctr

This solicitation totals seven hundred and fifty million rounds, most of which are hollow points.

These are just two examples of many similar solicitations including those for purchases of hollow points for departments such as Social Security Administration (174,000 rounds of .357 Sig jacketed hollow points) and National Oceanic Atmospheric Administration (46,000 round of hollow points).

Now let's look at the some recent orders for automatic assault weapons that the DHS has ordered.

Forbes.com March 13, 2012 reported:

> "First, we hear that DHS is in the process of stockpiling more than 1.6 billion rounds of hollow-point ammunition, along with 7,000 fully-automatic 5.56x45mm NATO "personal defense weapons" plus a huge stash of 30-round high-capacity magazines. Incidentally, those are also known as "assault weapons", but are not the limited single-fire per trigger-pull semi-automatic types that we civilians are currently allowed to own."

Another contract was awarded to a Virginia based firearms manufacturer, this time for $4.5 million worth of Heckler & Koch sub machine guns. This was in addition to an April 2012 deal (Solicitation Number: 20069404) with Heckler & Koch for $143,510 of UMP 40 submachine guns.

Remember, we are talking about the Department of Homeland Security who are buying these fully automatic assault rifles and submachine guns—not the U.S. Army or Marines. But it doesn't stop there.

Forbes.com also reported on the purchase of 2,717 Mine Resistant Armored Protection vehicles, they state:

> ". . . we find out that DHS, through the U.S. Army Forces Command, recently purchased and retrofitted 2,717 Mine-Resistant Armored Protection (MRAP) vehicles formerly used for counterinsurgency in Iraq. They are specifically designed to protect occupants from ambush attacks, incorporating bullet-proof windows designed to withstand small-arms fire, such as .223-caliber rifles . . . . DHS officer stationed in El Paso, Texas, proudly describing these mobile marauding marvels as: *"Mine-resistant . . . we use to deliver our teams to high-risk warrant services . . . [with] gun ports so we can actually shoot from within the vehicle; you may think it's pretty loud but actually it's not too bad . . . we have gun ports there in the back and two on the sides as well. They are designed for .50-caliber weapons."*

And to cap it off, the DHS has spent $2 Million with *Law Enforcement Targets Inc.* for shooting targets that include children and pregnant women as the primary target. The targets even have a title—'No More Hesitation". I'm not kidding.

INTERNET SEARCH TERM: DHS shooting targets pregnant women

By now if you do not believe something is very wrong you must surely be living in that river in Egypt—DENIAL.

The Department of Homeland Security, our government is gearing up for a battle and there are only two possible reasons that I can see.

1. They are expecting the United States homeland to come under massive ground force attack.
2. They are expecting massive civil unrest, martial law and quite possibly the second American Civil War.

Let's try and figure this out. On comes the raincoat, light the cigar and scratch your head. If I were Columbo I'd be asking this: If they were expecting a massive attack from Russia or China then why would they be doing everything in their power to disarm the American people?

So there's your answer. They are gearing up for massive civil unrest, martial law and possibly Civil War II. I believe Russian and Chinese troops will be used to clean up the mess several years later and claim territory in lieu of unpaid U.S. Debts.

The stage is set. The DHS is ready with ammo, weapons, armor and internment camps. The question remains, what will be the trigger? A total financial meltdown and economic collapse? A nuclear, chemical or biological *false flag* event? Perhaps even an Electro Magnetic Pulse (EMP) or a "natural" event such as devastating earthquake or solar flare.

In my first book I detailed how "they" (the satanic worshiping globalists) just love to use Television, Movies, books and video games to tell you what they are planning and with TV shows like *Revolution*, movies like *Red Dawn 2*, books like *One Second After* and video games like *Call Of Duty 2*—all of these depict scenarios of nationwide power failure mostly as a result of an EMP—I'm hoping I'm wrong.

Actually there is one more possibility to explain this build up of weapons and ammo by the DHS. We know it's possible for the communists to control assets inside the White House, Harry Dexter White was one example. But what if they managed to get a communist at the highest seat? What would be the main objectives for a covert communist President? Disarm the people, cripple our economy, debase religion and quite possibly this: create a re-supply of weapons and ammo for an incoming Russian attack, most likely while our regular troops attention is diverted to the Middle East and Korea. This might explain why Russian troops have been conducting drills using U.S. weapons—I see no other reason, do you?

Could that really be possible? Could we elect someone to the presidency without knowing their true identity? Let me answer that—Barry Soetoro. (see next chapter—Trojan Horse)

Before we discover who Barry Soetoro is, let's look at some of the preparations being made by Russia and the *New World Order* over the last few years.

July 12, 2010—Russia Today (RT.COM) announced that:

"Moscow Arms Against Nuclear Attack"

> "Nearly 5,000 new emergency bomb shelters will be built in Moscow by 2012 to save people in case of potential attacks.
>
> Moscow authorities say the measure is urgent as the shelters currently available in the city can house no more than half of its population."

This sent the *2012 End Of The World* theorist into high gear as this surely proved that Russia was planning for the end of the World on December 21, 2012, but as we know that date has come and gone, so did they waste their money or were they building these nuclear shelters for another reason?

It appears that the United States has also been busy building underground bases, transit systems and shelters too, but they are not for you and me—just the elite few who will be chosen when the time is right.

I do not have access to the detailed data to prove how many and exactly where they are by you can search for yourself and see the equipment they are using:

INTERNET SEARCH TERM: U.S. NUCLEAR TUNNEL
BORING MACHINES

It might also be of interest to know that in 2006 the Bill and Melinda Gates Foundation along with support from the Rockefeller Foundation and Warren Buffett spent $30 million on a "Doomsday Seed Vault" to be built on the remote island of Spitsbergen which belongs to Norway in the Barents Sea (about seven hundred miles from the North Pole). In the vault, named the Svaldbard Global Seed Vault, which is now "live" contains up to three million different varieties of seeds (all non Genetically Modified of course) and up over two billion seeds from the entire world, 'so that crop diversity can be conserved for the future.'

These sociopaths do not spend their wealth without good reason, so you have to wonder what they know is coming. Food for thought?

"I wrote *Dreams from my Father*."

—Bill Ayers

"The free market doesn't work, it's never worked."

—President Barack Obama

CHAPTER 6

The Trojan Horse

You don't have to understand Greek mythology to know that the term *Trojan Horse* is used when referring to a deception to allow a sneak attack from within. The term 5th *Column* is another often used to describe a group acting covertly within a much larger group or nation to bring it down. Is there evidence that we have a Trojan Horse or 5th Column operating within the United States?—absolutely!

The head figure of the Trojan Horse goes by the name Barry Soetoro, a.k.a. Frank Marshall Davis Jr., or perhaps better known as President Barack Hussein Obama.

The evidence for this claim is overwhelming, but so too is the subterfuge and cover up. I will now try and provide a concise summary that supports this claim.

When Sheriff Joe Arpaio's volunteer posse concluded their investigation into the claims that President Barack Obama was not born in Hawaii, but born in Kenya as was claimed, the evidence was conclusive and led Arpaio and his lead investigator to state that:

"The birth certificate is definitely forged!"

Now before you read any more, find a pen and grab your notebook and make a note of the date that Arpaio announced his findings—March 1, 2012

The PDF format of the long form birth certificate provided by the White House and the one that Obama had sworn to be the real certificate had at least eleven layers to it, which proves that it couldn't possibly be a simple photo copy.

Some elements of the birth certificate contained a font type that used a spacing technique called *Kerning*. *Kerning* is only available with computer word processing and was not a technique that was possible in 1961 using a standard typewriter.

A birth certificate for the *Nordyke* twins born at the same hospital one day after Obama's reported birth did not use a font type using *Kerning*.

Jerome Corsi, author of "Where's the Birth Certificate?" and World Net Daily writer details a report that Alan Hulton, a postman for thirty nine years, had come forward and said that he used to deliver mail to the home of Thomas and Mary Ayers (father of Weather Underground bomber Bill Ayers) and that Mary had told the postman that "they were helping a young black foreign student through schooling". The postman also recalls seeing Obama visiting the Ayres to "thank them for their help". Obama is also reported to tell the postman in 1989 that "he was going to be president". Alan Hulton made a sworn affidavit to Sheriff Arpaio on these points.

Former Hawaii elections clerk Tim Adams signed an affidavit swearing he was told by his supervisors in Hawaii that no long-form, hospital-generated birth certificate existed for Barack Obama in Hawaii and that neither Queens Medical Center or the Kapi'olani Medical Center in Honolulu had any record of Obama having been born in their medical facilities. Adams swears in the affidavit :

"I became aware that many requests were being made to the City and County of Honolulu Elections Division, the Hawaii Office of Elections, and the Hawaii Department of Health from around the country to obtain a copy of then-Senator Barack Obama's long-form, hospital-generated birth certificate. Senior officers in the City and County of Honolulu Elections Division told me on multiple occasions that no Hawaii long-form, hospital-generated birth certificate existed for Senator Obama in the Hawaii Department of Health . . . and there was no record that any such document had ever been on file in the Hawaii Department of Health or any other branch or department of the Hawaii government."

So the evidence proves that the birth certificate is forged, but what is the real reason for this? Let's explore.

Michelle Obama, during a speaking engagement said:

"When we took our trip to and visited his home country in Kenya . . ."

His grandmother is quoted as saying:

"The baby (Barack Hussein Obama) was born in Kenya and that shortly after he was born, Stanley Ann returned to Hawaii."

Some might say that this implies Obama was born in Kenya, however, in the excellent, must watch documentary "Dreams From My Real Father" by Joel Gilbert, it claims that Barack was indeed born in Hawaii, but his birth certificate was forged for another reason—to hide the identity of his real father.

The documentary provides very compelling evidence to show that Frank Marshall Davis was his real father and not the "Kenyan goat herder" that Obama claims.

This documentary shows Obama's mother, Stanley Ann Dunham was the daughter of CIA operative Stanley Dunham, or "Gramps" as Obama

45

refers to him. Stanley Dunham's assignments included monitoring known Communist Party members such as Frank Marshall Davis.

According to Paul Kengor Ph.D. in his book "The Communist"—

> "Here are the facts, and they are indisputable. Frank Marshal Davis was a pro-Soviet, pro Red-China, card carrying member of Communist Party USA (CPUSA). His Communist Party number was 47544."

The documentary "Dreams From My Real Father" details how he wrote for newspapers such as the Chicago Star and the Honolulu Record, espousing his anti capitalist and pro communist views. He was also the president of a camera club called the 'Lens Camera Club' and much of his photographic work was of nudes.

When Dunham was working in Hawaii at the same time Frank Marshall Davis was there, the young Ann Dunham struck up a very friendly relationship with Davis, seemingly to annoy her father. This included posing nude for Davis and ended up with her being pregnant.

Stanley Dunham could not allow Frank Marshall Davis to be listed as the father since this was one of the men he was supposed to be monitoring, therefore it was decided to state "Father Unknown" on the birth certificate. This was only a temporary measure and Stanley Dunham soon agreed terms with a black Kenyan he was monitoring by the name Barack (Beerick) Hussein Obama.

After a suitable time, Ann Dunham divorced Barrack Obama senior and in 1967 married an Indonesian named Lolo Soetoro.

Ann and Lolo moved to Jakarta, Indonesia where they changed her sons name to Barry Soetoro. On the Indonesian school application form Lolo Soetoro stated that Barry was an Indonesian Citizen and that his religion was Muslim.

That marriage broke up and Ann returned to Hawaii with her son Barry. Barry would often visit Frank Marshall Davis and indeed spent of his teenage years with "Uncle Frank", where he undoubtedly learnt the virtues of communism.

In 1979 Barry studied at Occidental College and was known as a revolutionary Marxist. Later he moved to New York City and 'studied' Political science at Columbia and it is there that he attended the MAY 19th Communist Organization, a subset of the Weather Underground, and met Bill Ayers.

The importance of his relationship with Bill Ayers will become more apparent in the next chapter "Weathermen".

However, it's interesting to note that on November 6, 2009 CBS News published an article titled:

"Did Barack Obama Actually Attend Columbia?"

In the article it includes a quote from Wayne Allen Root who was also studying political science at the same time as Obama:

> "I don't know a single person at Columbia that knew him, and they all know me." . . . Obama's photograph does not appear in the school's yearbook and Obama consistently declines requests to talk about his years at Columbia, provide school records, or provide the name of any former classmates or friends while at Columbia."

Despite his poor grades at Columbia, which is hardly a surprise given the above statements, he used the influence of Bill Ayers, Thomas Ayers (Bill's father) and Don Warden (also known as Khalid al Monsour) to get into Harvard Law School.

The association with the Ayers family continued and to support his run for office it was suggested that a biography which depicted the struggle of a Kenyan goat herders' son would be just the ticket. The biography "Dreams from my Father" was released and Bill Ayers (the known Weatherman terrorist) claims that he was the author.

The documentary also details Obama's/Barry's/Frank Marshall Davis Jr. association with the Chicago mafia, the Rhinoplasty (nose job) he had in an attempt to minimize his likeness to his real father and his association with Rev. Jeremiah Wright.

＊　＊　＊

As a reminder, in my first book I provided New York Post and MSNBC reports where Lynne Cheney (Dick Cheney's wife) admitted that Obama and Dick were distant cousins and that Obama was also related to George Bush and Prince Charles and hence Vlad the Impaler (a.k.a. Dracula).

Barry/Barrack/Frank Jr. is 9th cousin twice removed to Queen Elizabeth.

Please verify before continuing.

＊　＊　＊

So far we have explored the evidence that our President—the man who has primary control of the nuclear football and who would effectively become our legal dictator once the Executive Orders and Presidential Directives are given the excuse to be activated—may have a few skeletons in the closet. But is there anything else he is hiding in the closet?

On August 3, 2003 the New York Times published an article titled:

"Double Lives on the Down Low"

It provides details of an underground *club* known as "Down Low' which is primarily for black men who secretly engage in homosexual acts whilst presenting a *straight* appearance in public.

World Net Daily writer, Jerome Corsi Ph.D. published as article on October 2, 2012 titled:

"Trinity Church Member Reveal Obama Shocker"

In this article he provides details of the Down Low club and link to Obama via the matchmaking services of Rev. Jeremiah Wright and the Trinity United Church in Chicago. Corsi details how having a wife is simply *your beard* or cover, so that you appear to be straight, but really are not. Corsi quotes from a source known as Carolyn who said:

> "At Trinity, if you even hint at talking about Obama being gay, you were reminded of your dear departed choir director . . . he was killed and it wasn't a robbery"

The article details how two black homosexuals belonging to the Trinity United Church, where Obama attended, were shot and killed and a third died reportedly of septicemia, pneumonia and AIDS, all within a five week period at the end of 2007. Their names were, Donald young, Larry Bland and Nate Spencer.

Corsi's article also refers to "The Globe" tabloid who on July 17, 2010 published an interview with Norma Jean Young, the mother of Donald Young which stated:

> "What was the cause of my son's death? I'm very suspicious that it may have been related to Obama. Donald and Obama were very close friends. Whatever went on with this is very private . . . . I am suspicious of a cover-up!"

Is it a just a coincidence that these men died at the time Obama was pushing for the Democratic nomination for President. Do you think Obama would have been nominated if they spoke up about his alleged homosexuality?

✱ ✱ ✱

It certainly appears that being associated with top political people is not without risk. Or perhaps the following list represents just a string of tragic coincidences. I'll let you decide for yourself.

　　1—James McDougal—He was once a staunch supporter of Bill Clinton and defended his involvement in the Whitewater affair, however after being convicted he turned against Clinton making several serious allegations. He died of an apparent heart attack while in solitary confinement. CNN reported the following headlines on May 15, 1998—"James McDougal's Last Word is a Tell-All Book"

2—**Mary Caitrin Mahoney**—A former White House intern was murdered July 1997 at a Starbucks Coffee Shop in Georgetown. According to "The Judiciary report" March 20,2008 The murder happened just after she was to go public with her story of sexual harassment in the White House.

3—**Vince Foster**—Former White House councilor, and colleague of Hillary Clinton at Little Rock's Rose Law firm. Died of a gunshot wound to the head, ruled a suicide. The Daily Mail ran the following headlines on January 15, 2008—"The man who knew too much? The truth about the death of Hilary Clinton's closest friend Vince Foster."

4—**Ron Brown**—Secretary of Commerce and former DNC Chairman was reported to have died by impact in a plane crash. A pathologist close to the investigation reported that there was a hole in the top of Brown's skull resembling a gunshot wound. At the time of his death Brown was being investigated, and spoke publicly of his willingness to cut a deal with prosecutors. The rest of the people on the plane also died. A few days later the air Traffic controller committed suicide. WND.com writer Jack Cashill published an article on September 29, 2004 titled "The Assassination of Ron Brown" in which he states "The evidence strongly suggests that Ron Brown was in fact assassinated"

5—**C. Victor Raiser, II**—Raiser, died in a private plane crash in July 1992. The New York Times stated August 2, 1992 that "Dee Dee Myers, described him as "a major player" in the Clinton organization."

6—**Paul Tulley**—Democratic National Committee Political Director found dead in a hotel room in Little Rock , September 1992. He was described by Clinton as a "dear friend and trusted advisor". New York Times confirmed on September 25, 1992 that "He had moved to Little Rock this fall to aid in Gov. Bill Clinton's drive for the White House."

7—**Ed Willey**—Clinton fundraiser, found dead November 1993 deep in the woods in VA of a gunshot wound to the head. His death was ruled a suicide. Ed Willey died on the same day his wife Kathleen Willey claimed Bill Clinton groped her in the oval office in the White House. Ed Willey was involved in several Clinton fund raising events. On November 5, 2007 WND.com published an article titled "Kathleen Willey Suspects Clintons Murdered Husband"

8—**Jerry Parks**—was the head of Clinton's gubernatorial security team in Little Rock. He was gunned down in his car at a deserted intersection outside Little Rock Park's son said his father was building a dossier on Clinton . He allegedly threatened to reveal this information. After he died the files were mysteriously removed from his house. Prorev.com (Progressive Review) published an article titled "The strange death of Jerry Parks and the even stranger death of Dr David Millstein". August 23, 2006—"In September 1993, just two months after the death of Vince Foster, Clinton campaign security operative Jerry Parks was shot and killed in Little Rock in a gang style slaying. The story received virtually no attention save for a few journals including the Progressive Review. The murder remains unsolved. Now word comes that the man whom Park's widow, Lois Jane Parks, later married—Dr David Millstein—has also been murdered by an assailant with a knife and police are investigating."

9—**James Bunch**—Died from a gunshot suicide. It was reported that he had a "Black Book" of people which contained names of influential people who visited prostitutes in Texas and Arkansas. Source: WhatReallyHappened.com

10—**John Wilson**—Was found dead in May 1993 from an apparent hanging suicide. He was reported to have ties to Whitewater. Source: http://www.clintonmemoriallibrary.com/clintbodycnt.html

11—**Kathy Ferguson**—Ex-wife of Arkansas Trooper Danny Ferguson, was found dead in May 1994, in her living room with a gunshot to her head. It was ruled a suicide even though there were several packed suitcases, as if she were going somewhere. Danny Ferguson was a co-defendant along with Bill Clinton in the Paula Jones lawsuit, Kathy Ferguson was a possible corroborating witness for Paula Jones. Source: WhatReallyHappened.com

12—**Bill Shelton**—Arkansas State Trooper and fiancée of Kathy Ferguson. Critical of the suicide ruling of his fiancée, he was found dead in June, 1994 of a gunshot wound also ruled a suicide at the grave site of his fiancé. Source: WhatReallyHappened.com

13—**Gandy Baugh**—Attorney for Clinton's friend Dan Lassater, died by jumping out a window of a tall building January, 1994. "Mr. Lassater was a close associate of Gov. Clinton, and was later indicted on drug related charges, among other things. Baugh's law partner was "suicided" one month later on Feb. 9, 1994" Source:JCS-group.com

14—**Florence Martin**—Accountant & sub-contractor for the CIA, was related to the Barry Seal, Mena, Arkansas, airport drug smuggling case. She died of three gunshot wounds." At the time of her death she had the account numbers and PIN for a bank account in the Cayman's in the name of Barry Seal which held 1.4 million dollars. Immediately following her death, the money was moved to someplace in the Virgin Islands." Source: WhatReallyHappened.com

15—**Suzanne Coleman**—Reportedly had an affair with Clinton when he was Arkansas Attorney General. She died of a gunshot wound to the back of the head, but it ruled as suicide. She was pregnant at the time of her death. Source: WhatReallyHappened.com

16—**Paula Grober**—Clinton's speech interpreter for the deaf from 1978 until her death December 9, 1992. She died in a one car accident with her body found thirty three feet away. Source: WhatReallyHappened.com

17—**Danny Casolaro**—A reporter who was investigating several of the Clinton Scandals, was found dead in the bathtub of a hotel room in West Virginia on Aug. 10, 1991, with his wrists slit. He had earlier warned his family that his life was in danger and if he was found dead due to an apparent accident or suicide, not to believe it. Source: http://www.clintonmemoriallibrary.com/clintbodycnt.html

18—**Paul Wilcher**—Attorney investigating corruption at Mena Airport with Casolaro and the 1980 "October Surprise" BCCI and

INSLAW. He was found in his Washington DC apartment dead of unknown causes on June 22,1993. Source: etherzone.com

19—**Jon Parnell Walker**—was a Washington investigator who had been probing into the Whitewater case, of which Vince Foster may have harbored more undisclosed knowledge than anyone. Walker "jumped" out of a window from the 22nd floor of an apartment building on August 15th 1993. Source: http://www.apfn. org/apfn/itsdanger.htm

20—**Barbara Wise**—Commerce Department Staffer. She died November 29, 1996—As the scandals continued to swirl round the Commerce Department and most of all about John Huang, Barbara Wise was found dead in her locked office at the Department of Commerce, where she partially nude and covered with bruises. No cause of death has ever been announced. Oddly enough, following the discovery of her body, Bill Clinton made an unscheduled return to the white House from Camp David, claiming he needed a book of poetry in order to complete his inauguration speech. Source: http://rense.com/political/ clintonbodycount.htm

21—**Christine M Mirzayan**, Clinton intern killed on August 1 1998. In the publicity prior to the Paula jones law suit Newsweek revealed that "a former White House staffer" with the initial "M" was about to go public with a story about sexual harassment at the White House. Thereafter Christine was found beaten to death with a heavy object near Georgetown University, Washington. Source: http://www. russwill.com/library/politics/clinton/bloody_bill_clinton.htm

22—**Dr. Stanley Heard**—Chairman of the National Chiropractic Health Care Advisory Committee died with his attorney Steve Dickson in a small plane crash. Dr. Heard, in addition to serving on Clinton's advisory council, personally treated Clinton's mother, stepfather and brother. Source: http://www.morningliberty. com/2013/03/17/false-flag-911-philip-marshall-killed-to-silence-911-truth/

23—**Barry Seal**—Drug running pilot out of Mena Arkansas, his death was no accident. Linked to Bill Clinton (then Governor of Arkansas) and George H.W. Bush and the Iran Contra scandal. Source: http://www.ncoic.com/clinton.htm

24—**Johnny Lawhorn, Jr.**—Mechanic, found a check made out to Bill Clinton in the trunk of a car left at his repair shop. He was found dead after his car had hit a utility pole. Source: http://www. alipac.us/f9/bill-hillary-clinton-legacy-76659-print/

25—**Stanley Huggins**—Investigated Madison Guaranty Savings & Loan. He died June 24, 1994. Huggins specialized in working with banks and savings and loan associations and was in the spotlight in connection with the Whitewater Development Corp. probe involving President Clinton. Huggins headed an examination in 1987 into the loan practices of Madison Guaranty Savings and Loan and produced a 300 to 400 page report. His death was a purported suicide and his report was never released. Source: http://alamo-girl.com/0364.htm

26—**Hershell Friday**—Attorney and Clinton fund raiser died March 1, 1994 when his plane exploded. Source: http://rense.com/political/clintonbodycount.htm

27—**Kevin Ives & Don Henry**—Known as "The boys on the track" case. Reports say the boys may have stumbled upon the Mena Arkansas airport drug operation. Arkansas State Medical Examiner Fahmy Malak, appointed by Gov. Bill Clinton, quickly ruled the boys' deaths "accidental," saying they were unconscious or in a deep sleep as a result of smoking marijuana.

A second autopsy showed that Henry had been stabbed in the back and had been struck on the head before being placed on the tracks. Under public pressure over the official mishandling of the case from the beginning, Gov. Clinton called in two pathologists from out of state to review the work of the medical examiner and state crime lab where the autopsies were conducted. But when the Saline County grand jury tried to subpoena those experts for testimony, Clinton refused to allow it.

Many linked to the case died before their testimony could come before a Grand Jury. Source: http://www.wnd.com/1997/05/874/

THE FOLLOWING PERSONS HAD INFORMATION ON THE IVES/HENRY CASE:

28—**Keith Coney**—Died when his motorcycle slammed into the back of a truck, July 1988. Some reports indicated that he was being chased by an unidentified vehicle. Source: http://earlcallaway. com/corpsecount.html

29—**Keith McMaskle**—Died, stabbed 113 times, Nov, 1988. Filmmaker Pat Matrisciana's film, titled "Obstruction of Justice: The Mena Connection," examined the still-unsolved murders of Don Henry, Kevin Ives, and Keith McKaskle, along with some of what was known about corruption at the time in Saline County. Source: http://www.arktimes.com/arkansas/out-of-control-in-lonoke-county/Content?oid=864247

30—**Gregory Collins**—Claimed to have information on the Ives/ Henry case. He died from a gunshot blast to the face January 1989. Source: http://rense.com/political/clintoncount.htm

31—**Jeff Rhodes**—another person who claimed to have information about the Ives-Henry murders, was shot in the head. His burned body was found in the city dump, with his hands, feet, and head partially severed. Source: http://rense. com/political/clintoncount.htm

32—**James Milam**—Was found decapitated. However, the Coroner, Fahmy Malak, ruled his death was due to "natural causes". Source: http://www.spiritoftruth.org/arkncide.htm

33—**Jordan Kettleson**—Was found with shotgun blast to June 1990. He also had claimed to have information on the Ives/Henry Case. Source: http://rense.com/political/clintoncount.htm

34—**Richard Winters**—another person who claimed to have information about the Ives-Henry murders, was killed by a man using a sawed-off shotgun. Source: http://rense.com/political/ clintoncount.htm

THE FOLLOWING WERE BODYGUARDS FOR BILL CLINTON:

36—**Major William S. Barkley, Jr.** Died May 20, 1993. According to NY Times "One of several military helicopters in the Presidential fleet crashed today, killing all four crew members aboard, the authorities said"

37—**Captain Scott J. Reynolds**—Died in the same crash as above

38—**Sgt. Brian Haney**—Died in the same crash as above

39—**Sgt. Tim Sabel**—Died in the same crash as above. According to source: http://www.freewebs.com/jeffhead/liberty/liberty/bdycount.txt

All had escorted Clinton on flight to the U.S.S. Roosevelt and a video tape made by firemen at crash site seized by feds.

40—**Major General William Robertson**—died: 2/23/93—he was killed when their Army UH-60 Blackhawk helicopter crashed in Wiesbaden, Germany. No cause was ever determined.—V Corps figured prominently in the US Bosnia-Serbia peacekeeping operations, along with the carrier U.S.S. Roosevelt. Source: http://whatreallyhappened.com/RANCHO/POLITICS/BODIES.html

41—**Col. William Densberger**—As above

42—**Col. Robert Kelly**—As above

43—**Spec. Gary Rhodes**—As above

The following four men were killed by gunfire in the Waco, Texas, assault on the Branch Davidians. All four were examined by a "private doctor" and died from nearly identical wounds to the left temple, so-called execution style. In his address to employees of the Treasury Department in the Cash Room on March 18, 1993, Clinton said: "My prayers and I'm sure yours are still with the families of all four of the Alcohol, Tobacco and Firearms agents who were killed in Waco". Source for next four: http://www.theforbiddenknowledge.com/hardtruth/clintonbodycount.htm

44—**Steve Willis**—Clinton bodyguard Died Feb. 28, 1993
45—**Robert Williams**—Clinton bodyguard Died Feb. 28, 1993
46—**Conway LeBleu**—Clinton bodyguard Died Feb. 28, 1993
47—**Todd McKeehan**—Clinton bodyguard Died Feb. 28, 1993

the ATF confirmed that all four had at one point been bodyguards for Bill Clinton, three while he was campaigning for President, and while he had been governor of Arkansas. Source: http://whatreallyhappened.com/RANCHO/POLITICS/BODIES.html

I'm sure you'll agree that's quite some list, but according to Rense.com—

"The CLINTON BODY COUNT has climbed to 85 seriously DEAD people connected with that adorable William Jefferson Clinton, (born 'Billy Blythe')"

Source: http://rense.com/political/clintonbodycount.htm

Note to self: Remind me not to get too close to Bill and Hillary and I should probably cancel that dinner date with them. Oh and don't get on any military helicopters anytime soon.

If you want to further research the alleged CIA drug running through Mena, Arkansas while Clinton was Governor of the state, I suggest a couple of very well documented books:

The Medusa File—Craig Roberts

Powderburns—Cocaine, Contras, & the Drug War—Celerino Castillo III

Now returning to Barry/FMD/Barrack, should we really be concerned with all this fuss about who is Obama's real father is and his connections with Communist Terrorist? Especially when:

Christian News Network, January 21, 2013: Newsweek Hails Obama as Messianic 'Second Coming'?

And

Media Research Center (MRC.org) May, 9 2011: "He's sort of God. He's going to bring all different sides together."

And

Danish newspaper Politiken: December 28, 2009, which stated, "Obama is, of course, greater than Jesus."

At least Obama denies these claims:

> "Contrary to rumors, I was not born a manger" but then he went on "I was actually born on Krypton and sent here to save the planet earth".

With lines like that I guess if he quits being president he can become a standup comedian—providing he's allowed a tele-prompter and joke writer.

Lastly, in wrapping up this chapter let's hear what Trunews radio host, Rick Wiles had to say on his show, March 20 2012

> "Think about the absurdity of the news. We have President Obama who looks like Lucifer in "the Bible" TV series, he's got flies swirling around his face like Beelzebub, Lord of the Flies. A biblical plague of tens of millions of locusts is descended into Israel just days before he arrived. His secret service codename is *Renegade* and his limousine is nicknamed *the Beast*. What more do I need to say?"

"In countries long accustomed to democracy, the empire of those oligarchies may be concealed behind democratic forms."

—Bertrand Russell, The Scientific Outlook, 1931

"A Presidential candidate may be "drafted" in response to "overwhelming popular demand", but it is well known that his name may be decided upon by half a dozen men sitting around a table in a hotel room."

—Edward Bernays, Propaganda, 1928

CHAPTER 7

Weathermen

Larry Grathwohl was a Law Enforcement agent working in Cincinnati, Ohio who volunteered to infiltrate the Weather Underground terrorist organization in 1969. His role within the Weather Underground was to carry directives from the central committee to the operating units in the field. What he discovered should have made the headlines around the World.

In a documentary interview filmed in 1982 titled "No Place to Hide—the Strategy and Tactics of Terrorism", Larry Grathwohl explained that the Weather Underground, or Weathermen, as they become known, received training in Cuba and received communications from the Tri Continental group who in turn was funded by the DGI (Cuban police), a known KGB supported and controlled organization. During his interview he stated the following:

> "I brought up the subject of what's going to happen after we take over the government? We become responsible for administrating two hundred and fifty million people. And there was {sic} no answers. No one had given any thought to economics, how you're going to clothe and feed these

people. The only thing that I could get was that they expected that the Cubans and the North Vietnamese and the Chinese and the Russians would all want to occupy different portions of the United States. They also believed that their immediate responsibility would be to protect against what they called the counter revolution and they felt this counter revolution could best be guarded against by creating and establishing re-education centers in the Southwest. Where we would take all the people that needed to be re-educated into the new way of thinking and teach them how things were going to be. I asked, well what is going to happen to those people who we can't re-educate, that are die-hard capitalists? And the reply was that they'd have to be eliminated and when I pursued this further they estimated that they would have to eliminate twenty five million people in these re-education centers. And when I say eliminate I mean kill twenty five million people. I want you to imagine sitting in a room with twenty five people most of which have graduate degrees from Columbia and other well known educational centers and hear them figuring out the logistics for the elimination of twenty five million people, and they were dead serious."

The Weathermen's stated aims was "A revolutionary organization of Communist men and women . . . . our goal is the destruction of U.S. imperialism and the achievement of a classless state. World Communism."

The Weathermen were founded on the Ann Arbor Campus of the University of Michigan. During the early 1970's they were responsible for several bombings including the United States Capitol, the Pentagon and New York City Police headquarters. Members of the Weathermen and May 19th Communist Organization (the same organization Obama joined) were involved in the Brinks armed robbery.

One of the founders of the Weathermen was William (Bill) Ayers. He and his wife, Bernadine Dohrn, were involved in some of the bombings, but because of illegal evidence gathering activities by the authorities, all charges were dropped. Bill Ayers is quoted in the New York Times, September 11, 2011 as saying:

> "I don't regret setting bombs," Bill Ayers said. "I feel we didn't do enough."

The same article asks:

> "So, would Mr. Ayers do it all again, he is asked? "I don't want to discount the possibility," he said."

This is where it get's interesting and ties in with earlier chapters. In an article posted June 4, 2012 on Brietbart.com is states:

Exclusive—The Vetting—Senator Barack Obama Attended Bill Ayers Barbeque, July 4 2005

The article reports that Dr. Tom Perrin, who was assistant professor of English at Huntingdon College in Montgomery, Alabama. He was a graduate of the University of Chicago and lived next door to bill Ayers and Bernadine Dohrn in Hyde Park. He posted the following on his blog at 8:44 a.m. on July 6, 2005:

> "Guess what? I spent the 4th of July evening with star Democrat Barack Obama! Actually, that's a lie. Obama was at a barbecue at the house next door (given by a law professor who is a former member of the Weather Underground) and we saw him over the fence at our barbecue. Well, the others did. It had started raining and he had gone inside be the time I got there. Nevertheless."

The article added:

> "Obama's presence—as a U.S. Senator—at the Ayers barbecue has been confirmed by another source, who told Breitbart News: "I too saw Obama at a picnic table in the Ayers/ Dohrn backyard, munching away—on the 4th of July.""

Another Brietbart.com article with the title:

Ayers and Obama: What the media hid

It detailed how:

> "Various boards on which Obama sat in the late 90s granted nearly $2 million dollars to Bill Ayers' Small Schools Workshop."

And

> "In addition to donations to Ayers' Small Schools Workshop group, the same foundations donated $761,100 to a related group run by Ayers' brother, John Ayers. In fact, in 2001 Obama would join the "leadership council" of a successor to the CAC called the Chicago Public Education Fund. Also on the leadership council of the group was Bill Ayers' brother John."

* * *

Having just provided some information from Brietbart.com it's worth digressing for a few moments to remember what happened to Andrew Brietbart.

Andrew Brietbart died suddenly at the age of forty three on March 1, 2012. According to the Coroner's office for the County of Los Angeles the autopsy performed on March 2 recorded his death as "natural", caused by heart failure and more specifically:

"Hypertrophic Cardiomyopathy with focal coronary atherosclerosis"

The toxicology report detailed that no prescription drugs were detected and that blood alcohol was .04%

Now check your notepad. Earlier I had asked you to write down the date of Sheriff Joe Arpaio's announcement that Obama's birth certificate was forged—it was March 1, 2012—the same day Brietbart dies.

The autopsy report was released on April 20 2012, and on the same day that the L.A. County forensic technician, Michael Cormier died of arsenic poisoning.

As reported in the L.A. Times April 28, 2012

> "At this point we haven't ruled out foul play," said Lt. Alan Hamilton of the Los Angeles Police Department. "It is one of the things being considered. We are waiting for the coroner's results."

Were Brietbart and Cormier silenced for a specific reason? Well, take a look at the following report:

International Business Times , May 2, 2012

> "Just a few weeks before his death, Breitbart had told an audience at a CPAC rally that he was in possession of video tapes of President Obama in college. Breitbart claimed that these tapes would incriminate the President. I've got videos . . . from his college days, to show you why racial division and class warfare are central to what 'hope' and 'change' was sold in 2008, Breitbart told the crowd. The rest of us slept while they plotted, and they plotted, and they plotted."

To conclude this section it's worth remembering that Stanislav Lunev, the highest ranking Soviet officer who defected to the West and several others have openly talked about assassination techniques that include the use of poisons, heart stopping drugs and cancer weapons to take out potential threats. And you can guarantee that the CIA, NSA, MI5, MI6 and other such agencies are more than capable of the same.

"America is like a healthy body and it's resistance is threefold: its patriotism, its morality and its spiritual life. I we can undermine these three areas, America will collapse from within."

—Joseph Stalin

CHAPTER 8

Communist Goals— New World Order Minions

For over two hundred years the United States has been the thorn in the side of the New World Order—the satanic worshiping bloodline of the European royals. Their stated goal of a One World Government, One World Religion and the vision as depicted in Aldous Huxley's *Brave New World* cannot become a reality whilst the citizens of United Stated stand strong. They have known this for many years. Carroll Quigley who studied the machinations of the Milner Group, Round Table, Royal Institute of International Affairs and the Council On Foreign Relations (CFR) confirmed in his book, "The Anglo-American Establishment", that after World War I, 'the Round Table group were busy with problems like the League of Nations and the United States'. Of course they were, it was hard enough to get the United States embroiled in the War, so they knew they would have to work very hard to convince Americans that a One World government was in their best interest. But that didn't stop them trying, they even attempted a Fascist coup in 1934 (Research General Smedley Butler), but ultimately they have understood that for the most part the Fabian Socialist technique using incremental steps would win versus revolution. It's only when they need to make really big leaps in change do they engineer a much bigger crisis or event. With this knowledge they have used scientific techniques and the Communist movement to accomplish their multi generational plan.

It's a multi generational plan to subvert the morals, values, spirit and culture of an entire nation. And I'm afraid to say that they've done a very good job of it. However, they may have won several battles, but the war is not over. This great country still has many great patriots who have not been chemically lobotomized and this is one of the reason why I chose to become an American Citizen and join in the Resistance.

By understanding their tactics and goals we can develop our own response and battle plan. So at this point it is worth detailing the forty five stated goals of the Communists as laid out in W. Cleon Skousens' 1958 book "The Naked Communist"—remember that these are Communist goals from over fifty years ago and many have likely changed or new goals added as time and technology moves on. Remember too that behind these Communist goals are the much larger goals of the satanic worshiping globalist who are simply using Communism as a tool to shape and bring about their vision.

Communist Goals

1. U.S. acceptance of coexistence as the only alternative to atomic war.
2. U.S. willingness to capitulate in preference to engaging in atomic war.
3. Develop the illusion that total disarmament by the United States would be a demonstration of moral strength.
4. Permit free trade between all nations regardless of Communist affiliation and regardless of whether or not items could be used for war.
5. Extension of long-term loans to Russia and Soviet Satellites.
6. Provide American aid to all nations regardless of Communist domination.
7. Grant recognition of Red China. Admission of Red China to the U.N.

8. Set up East and West Germany as separate states in spite of Khrushchev's promise in 1955 to settle the Germany question by free elections under supervision of the U.N.
9. Prolong the conferences to ban atomic tests because the U.S. has agreed to suspend tests as long as negotiations are in progress.
10. Allow all Soviet satellites individual representation in the U.N.
11. Promote the UN as the only hope for mankind. If the charter is rewritten, demand that it be set up as a one-world government with its own independent armed forces.
12. Resist any attempts to outlaw the Communist Party.
13. Do away with loyalty oaths.
14. Continue giving Russia access to the U.S. Patent office.
15. Capture one or both of the political parties in the United States.
16. Use technical decisions of the courts to weaken basic American institutions by claiming their activities violate civil rights.
17. Get control of the schools. Use them as transmission belts for socialism and current Communist propaganda. Soften the curriculum. Get control of teachers association. Put the party line in textbooks.
18. Gain control of all student newspapers.
19. Use student riots to foment public protests against programs or organizations which are under Communist attack.
20. Infiltrate the press. Get control of book-review assignments, editorial writing, policy-making positions.
21. Gain control of key positions in radio, TV and motion pictures.
22. Continue discrediting American culture by degrading all forms of artistic expression.
23. Control art critics and directors of art museums.—Promote ugliness, repulsive and meaningless art.
24. Eliminate all laws governing obscenity by calling them "censorship" and a violation of free speech and free press.
25. Break down cultural standards of morality by promoting pornography and obscenity in books, magazines, motion pictures, radio and TV.
26. Present homo-sexuality, degeneracy and promiscuity as "normal, natural, healthy".

27. Infiltrate the churches and replace revealed religion with "social" religion. Discredit the Bible and emphasize the need for intellectual maturity which does not need a "religious crutch".

28. Eliminate prayer or any phase of religious expression in the schools on the ground that it violates the principle of "separation of church and state".

29. Discredit the American Constitution by calling it inadequate, old-fashioned, out of step with modern needs, a hindrance to cooperation between nations on a world-wide basis.

30. Discredit the American founding fathers. Present them as selfish aristocrats who had no concern for the 'common man".

31. Belittle all forms of American culture and discourage the teaching of American history on the ground that it was only a minor part of "the big picture". Give more emphasis to Russian history since the Communist took over.

32. Support any socialist movement to give centralized control over any part of the culture-education, social agencies, welfare programs, mental health clinics etc.

33. Eliminate all laws or procedures which interfere with the operation of the Communist apparatus.

34. Eliminate the House Committee on Un-American Activities.

35. Discredit and eventually dismantle the FBI.

36. Infiltrate and gain control of more unions.

37. Infiltrate and gain control of big business.

38. Transfer some of the powers of arrest from the police to social agencies. Treat all behavioral problems as psychiatric disorders which no one but psychiatrists can understand or treat.

39. Dominate the psychiatric profession and use mental health laws as a means of gaining coercive control over those who oppose communist goals.

40. Discredit the family as an institution. Encourage promiscuity and easy divorce.

41. Emphasize the need to raise children away from the negative influence of parents. Attribute prejudices, mental blocks and retarding of children to suppressive influence of parents.

42. Create the impression that violence and insurrection are legitimate aspects of the American tradition; that students and

special-interest groups should rise up and use "united force' to solve economic, political or social problems.

43. Overthrow all colonial governments before native populations are ready for self government.
44. Internationalize the Panama Canal.
45. Repeal the Connally Reservation so the U.S. cannot prevent World Court from seizing jurisdiction over domestic problems. Give the World Court jurisdiction over nations and individuals alike.

There you have it, the stated goals of the Communist as a plan to take down the United States from within.

Now let's look at some examples to show how they have achieved the majority of their goals.

First on the issue of our nuclear arsenal. Just a few months after Obama is caught in an "open microphone incident" where he is seen glad handing Russian President Medvedev and telling him:

> "On all these issues, particularly on missile defense, this, this
> can be solved but it's important for him to give me space,"

We then see reports in the media about Obama's plans to significantly reduce our nuclear weapons.

Newsmax.com on March 21, 2013 reported the following:

Obama's Nuclear Weapons Drawdown Could Run Afoul of the Law

> "President Barack Obama's efforts to significantly curtail U.S.
> nuclear weapons without seeking the proper Senate approval
> are at best misguided and worst illegal, sources tell Newsmax.
>
> Obama is exploring opportunities to achieve the reductions in
> infrastructure and capability he seeks—including a drawdown
> to 1,000 weapons—without seeking the advice and consent of
> the Senate that international treaties require.

> Efforts to push the boundaries of the New Strategic Arms
> Reduction Treaty (New START) with Russia are ill-advised,
> sources say."

As I detailed in my first book, the East-West trade agreement in 1966
allowed equipment, including materials vital to the North Vietnamese
war effort to be traded to Russia and then on to North Vietnam. Since
then the United States has continued trading with Communist countries
including critical infrastructure materials and goods, such as aircraft as
reported in "The Atlantic Wire", January 20, 2011

> "In a press conference with Chinese President Hu Jintao on
> Wednesday, President Obama announced a slew of bilateral
> trade deals that will ramp up U.S. exports to China by over $45
> billion. Obama said the 70 deals—which include a $19 billion
> contract for 200 Boeing airplanes and $2 billion worth of clean
> energy, aviation, and railway joint ventures between GE and its
> Chinese partners"

What does the United States get in return? Billions of cheap plastic
crap to amuse us for two or three weeks before it falls apart. Fair trade?
Hardly.

On the issue of loans to Communist countries. The United States "fed
as many as ten million persons a day" to Russia in 1922 following the
Bolshevik Revolution, according to Carroll Quigley in his book "Tragedy
and Hope".

During the so called "Cold War" the United States and Canada provided
the Soviets which millions of tons of underpriced grains as is detailed in
Gary Allen's "The Rockefeller File":

> "Whether he fully realizes it or not, President Ford has put his
> stamp of approval on Secretary of State Henry Kissinger's
> grand design foreign policy for the establishment of a loosely
> knit world government before the end of the 1970s . . .

By calling for the development of a global strategy and policy for food and oil within the structure of the United Nations, the President clearly signaled his acceptance of the "new international order" being sought by Kissinger . . . .

Agriculture Secretary Earl Butz admitted of the proposed food bank that "in the end it will be the American taxpayer who pays for it." Who else? And the fact that worldwide distribution of our food will inevitably create food shortages and skyrocketing prices in America has not been overlooked by the Rockefeller conspirators. That is part of the plan . . . .

While US reserves of food and feed grains are already being depleted, Russia and Communist China have quietly been using part of their massive purchases of bargain-priced American grain to build up their stockpiles. Crews of US and foreign ships carrying US grain to Russian and Chinese ports have been told by Communist dock workers that every third or fourth shipment of US grain is being placed in permanent storage facilities as part of those countries' national reserve."

More recently and despite our national debt, much of which is actually loaned to us by China and Russia, we still find incredible reports of the U.S. Department of Energy (and ultimately the U.S. Taxpayer) providing loans to a Russian billionaire:

Forbes.com November 29, 2011—Russian Billionaire Awarded controversial energy Dept. Loan

"Just two months after the bankruptcy filing for publicly-financed solar-panel manufacturer Solyndra, controversy swirls around the latest questionable loan coming from the U.S. Department of Energy. This time, the $730 million loan was given to Russian billionaire Alexei Mordashov's steel manufacturer Severstal North America."

Several of the Communist goals were based on promoting the United Nations and allowing other Communist countries to join the U.N., well if

I had to score them on these it would have to be A++, do you remember these headlines from March 8, 2012:

Infowars.com—Coup D'etat: Pentagon & Obama Declare Congress Ceremonial

> "During a Senate Armed Services Committee hearing yesterday, Panetta and Joint Chiefs of Staff Chairman Gen. Martin Dempsey brazenly admitted that their authority comes not from the U.S. Constitution, but that the United States is subservient to and takes its marching orders from the United Nations and NATO, international bodies over which the American people have no democratic influence.

> Panetta was asked by Senator Jeff Sessions, "We spend our time worrying about the U.N., the Arab League, NATO and too little time, in my opinion, worrying about the elected representatives of the United States. As you go forward, will you consult with the United States Congress?"

> The Defense Secretary responded "You know, our goal would be to seek international permission. And we would come to the Congress and inform you and determine how best to approach this, whether or not we would want to get permission from the Congress."

What about our school system? We have a "no child left behind policy" that drags everyone down to the lowest level and which incidentally was introduced by the Republicans and George W. Bush and now under Obama we have the following report on March 22, 2013

The Sleuth Journal.com—Texas Public School Curriculum Teaches Students To Design A Socialist Flag And That Christianity Is A Cult

Here's one of the tasks children were given.

> "Notice socialist/communist nations use symbolism on their flags representing various aspects of their economic system.

> Imagine a new socialist nation is creating a flag and you
> have been put in charge of creating a flag. Use symbolism to
> represent aspects of socialism/communism on your flag. What
> kind of symbolism/colors would you use?"

At what point should we expect our teachers, those that are helping to mould our children's minds, push back and say "No! I will not teach this Communist crap! "? This definitely crossed the line.

This tactic also counts as an assault on patriotism, but they don't stop there. I challenge you to use the Youtube search term: FEMA Founding Fathers were terrorists.

You will find a video from 2001 that shows a FEMA 'educator' explaining to a group of police and firefighters that the Founding Fathers were the first terrorist organization in the United States.

Another goal was for Russia to continue with its access to the U.S. Patent Office. Again they have surpassed that as this headline in Newsmax, March 11, 1999 shows:

Scientist: Clinton Administration Gave China Top Nuclear Secrets

> "A nuclear weapons scientist, who has sought anonymity "to
> keep my position and keep supporting my family," has informed
> NewsMax.com that the Clinton administration has, in fact,
> aggressively sought to provide China with some of the nation's
> most closely guarded nuclear weapons technology.
>
> It seems like every day there are more and more Chinese at
> Livermore," he stated. The scientist said the administration
> had facilitated the transfer of laser technology employed in the
> process of making nuclear weapons-grade plutonium."

Over the last couple of decades our manufacturing jobs have been shipped off shore and why is that? For a start there are huge tax breaks given by our government (don't forget this is our taxes at work)

Providence Journal, September 27, 2010—"The law, right now, permits companies that close down American factories and offices and move those jobs overseas to take a tax deduction for the costs associated with moving the jobs to China or India or wherever."

Secondly it's because it is a fundamental policy of the New World Order. In his book "The True Story of the Bilderberg Group", Daniel Estulin devotes a chapter to proving how the J.P. Morgan and John D. Rockefeller gang—part of the same gang of international bankers responsible for the creation of our privately owned, run for profit central bank known as the Federal Reserve—used American tax payer money to support the Soviets. He includes a June 10, 1932 quote from Congressmen Louis McFadden:

> "Open up the books of Amtorg, the trading organization of the Soviet government in New York, and of Gostorg, the general office of the Soviet Trade organization, and of the State Bank of the Union of Soviet Socialist Republics, and you will be staggered to see how much American money has been taken from the United States Treasury for the benefit of Russia. Find out what business has been transacted for the State Bank of Soviet Russia by its correspondent, the Chase Bank of New York."

Although this is the first time I've mentioned the Bilderberg Group, I recommend you do your research and Estulins' book is a great starting point.

Continuing—As I reported in my first book, we have our schools telling children to remove the word "God" from poems, in support of Communist goal number twenty eight.

Despite the so called "War on terror" we continue to have wide open borders with Mexicans and other nationalities flooding into the United States. Yes, of course Border Control does stop some, after all they have to keep up the illusion that we are doing something, but this again is part of the plan. The more illegal immigrants, the closer the United States moves towards a population that is totally dependent on the government.

Illegal immigrants are not only taking jobs away from Americans, including jobs that college students would normally do to help pay for tuition—this is another tactic, keep the students poor and unable to pay for loans and therefore they too become reliant on the government—but they are also getting free health care, not paying taxes and yet many are being allowed to register to vote. And who do you think they vote for? The most socialist candidate on the ballot. This is why Obama is so keen to push through illegal immigrant reforms.

Let's briefly look at how homo-sexuality and moral degeneracy has become the norm in our society. For decades now the New World Orders' weapon of choice, the Television, has been flooding us with "characters" that are openly homo-sexual—I will refrain from using the word 'gay' because changing the meaning of words is another tactic they use—telling us that this is "normal, natural and healthy". They are following the script better than Obama reads off the teleprompter.

Another perfect example of this can be found in the headline from:

Fox News—Middle School Anti-Bullying Lesson Includes Lesbian Role Play, April 18, 2013

> "Young girls at a New York middle school were instructed to ask one another for a lesbian kiss and boys were given guidance on how to tell if women are sluts during an anti-bullying presentation on gender identity and sexual orientation, angry parents allege . . . . Parents are especially furious after their young daughters were told that it was perfectly normal for 14-year-old girls to have sex and there was nothing their parents could do to intervene."

Communist Goal number twenty six—check.

It didn't take them long to check off goal thirty four. The House Committee on Un-American Activities had a name change in 1969 to "House Committee on Internal Security" and finally in 1975 under President Gerald Ford it was abolished.

Are you seeing how this works? A change in the name to reduce its impact and then continue over time to chip away and make it less relevant before doing away with it totally.

Do you also think it's just a coincidence that Obama has appointed so many "Czars", including John Holdren, our *Science Czar* who in his 1977 book Ecoscience—Population, Resources, Environment, suggested putting sterilants in our water supply. Or what about John Brennan, our *Terrorism Czar*, who has suggested disbanding the U.S. Military. Or perhaps your favorite is Cass Sunstein, our *Regulatory Czar* who doesn't like the idea of free speech and private gun ownership?

Whist we are on the subject of private gun ownership, let's review the United Nation Arms Trade Treaty. Now remember that the United Nations was established at the end of World War II by the same group of Central Bankers that have engineered and manipulated all major wars in at least the last one hundred years (as detailed in my first book) and that the land for the United Nations building in New York City was donated by none other than David Rockefeller. So let's understand that the United Nations is a major organization of the *globalists*. Whilst this treaty may appear on the surface as innocent and not an infringement on individual rights to bear arms, when you look under the covers you'll see that it only recognizes the right of the State, not the individual.

With regards to private ownership it states in the preamble of the treaty:

> "Lawful private ownership and the use of conventional arms exclusively for, inter alia [among other things], recreational, cultural, historical and sporting activities for States where such ownership and use are permitted or protected by law."

Notice that it does not include private gun ownership for the purposes of self defense and for militia's guarding against a tyrannical government.

Now let's look at a statement made by our Marxist Communist leader on a visit to Denver, Colorado on April 3, 2013 and as reported in the Denver Blaze:

Obama: Gun Control Won't Lead to confiscation Because "I am Constrained by a System Our Founders put In Place"

Now remember what Defense Secretary, Penetta and the Joint Chief of Staff Chairman, General Martin Dempsey said in March 2012, detailed earlier in this chapter—they take their orders from the U.N. and NATO, not Congress.

By United States law even though the President can and has signed this treaty it must still be ratified in the Senate. At the time of writing this, that has not happened. Therefore, I suggest that if it appears that the Senate does not have enough votes to make this treaty legal, then we can expect another *Batman* or *Sandy Hook* event to ensure public outrage and enough Senators will change their mind and vote. This is their modus operandi and they stick with it.

Another globalist/Communist goal is to make everyone dependent on the government and you only have to look at the "Obama Care" health laws to understand that this is a major part of their agenda. You will be forced to purchase insurance and forced to take their death sentence vaccines. Small American companies will be forced out of business as they are unable to compete with the larger globalist corporations, many whom are exempt from the taxes and restrictions being put on the smaller companies. This will further consolidate power into the few, reduce competition and ultimately result in the Communization of the United States.

Need I continue? Well let me finish with these three examples and reports:

Fox News, October 1, 2009—Empire State Building Goes Red for Communist China, Sparking Protest

> "The Empire State Building shone in red and yellow lights over New York City on Wednesday night to celebrate the 60th anniversary of the bloody communist takeover."

Rense.com, December 10, 1999—Red China: Gatekeeper of the Panama Canal—Missile Crisis Coming?

> "Jimmy Carter never would have been able to ran through his two treaties giving away our Panama Canal if the Senate in 1978 could have looked into the future and known that, when the U.S. Flag is lowered on December 31, 1999, Red China would become its gatekeeper. But that's what's scheduled to happen unless Congress takes immediate action to prevent it."

Congress did not prevent it.

New York Times, December 31, 1999—Panama Canal Sees the Last of the Stars and Stripes

> "The last American flag was lowered at the Panama Canal today; for the first time since the United States completed the waterway in 1914, the Stars and Stripes will no longer fly over it."

Communist goal number forty four—Completed.

World Net Daily, December 9, 2012—Obama's Money Plans Backed by Communists

"The Communist Part USA is backing Barack Obama's position on the coming fiscal cliff and claims its economic program "will unfold in the coming year" with the reelection of Obama and continued Democrat control of the U.S. Senate."

These examples are just the tip of the iceberg in my attempt to prove to you that the United States is at a tipping point. We cannot rely on "HOPE" anymore; otherwise we could well face this greeting:

"Welcome comrade to the American Soviet Socialist Republic!"

How does this sit in your stomach—it's time to do something! It's time to make a stand and resist!

"The biggest mistake of the West has been allowing itself to drift into a state of mental stagnation, apathy and inaction. In some circles, motivations of patriotism, loyalty and the traditional dreams of 'freedom for all men' have been lying dormant or have been paralyzed by a new kind of strange thinking."

—W. Cleon Skousen,
The Naked Communist, 1958

CHAPTER 9

Summary

At the very beginning of this book I provided some of the lyrics from the rock band, Snow Patrol, which was from a track titled "Open Your Eyes". I hope that this book has gone some way in doing that for you. Before I conclude with a positive look at what we must do to change direction it's worth taking a deep breath and summarizing what I have presented so far in this book.

I believe I have proven beyond doubt that plans and procedures are in place for Civilian labor camps on U.S. soil to be filled following a major event or other catastrophic failure of the system. The Executive Orders and Presidential Directives have been signed and given the right set of engineered (or natural) circumstances, are ready to propel our President into the position of dictator with no congressional oversight.

I have detailed how the Department of Homeland Security is preparing for a fight and it's a fight they expect to have with us, otherwise why would they want us disarmed? It's a fight in which they will use scientifically selected psychopaths and foreign troops to wage war against the Citizens of the United States. Again we should remember that Russian troops have been training within the United States using American weapons.

I have provided one possibility for a scenario that could trigger the announcement of Martial Law and the enactment of the Executive Orders. A nuclear bomb or several nuclear bombs exploding simultaneously in the United States is one of the scenario's we've looked at based on the *predictive programming* and the efforts our mainstream media pushes with the idea that the North Koreans are planning such an attack. This all seems a bit too coincidental to me.

FOX NEWS, March 29, 2013—

> " Shortly after midnight local time, North Korean state television reported that Kim signed orders to put the nation's rockets on combat-ready status. In a photo released on state-run media, a chart titled "U.S. mainland strike plan" could be seen and a map showed missiles arcing into Hawaii, Washington, Los Angeles and Austin, Texas."

Seriously, who are they kidding? But I guess we do need another *boogey man* to scare us all, especially now that Osama is officially dead.

Just like the magician, when the left hand is waving you know you should be focusing your attention on the right hand.

This is just one of the many plans they have and are considering. Another option is a global economic collapse that will be much worse than the Great Depression and if they follow their normal play book, it will result in the Third World War, after which they will provide their solution to an exhausted and depleted population.

I have provided the evidence that at best we have a liar and a fraud as President and almost definitely a Marxist Communist who, along with a willing media, has conducted a campaign of subterfuge to cover up his real identity and therefore his real agenda.

Lastly, I challenge anyone to deny that the Communist goals as highlighted in 1958 have not only been met, but in most cases have been far exceeded.

The future of the United States and therefore the entire World hangs in the balance. If humanity is to avoid the satanic plans of the New World Order we have to take immediate actions. The final chapter identifies a forty five step plan to do that.

"It's *our* ride and *our* choice of where we want it to go. This is what the manipulators have worked so hard to keep from us. But the truth is out and the genie is free and what we do with this knowledge is now our own responsibility. We can change the world or we can run and hide . . . it's just a choice between fear and love . . . enjoy the ride"

—David Icke, The David Icke guide
to the Global Conspiracy (and how to end it)

"When the influence which the Institute [Royal Institute of International Affairs] wields is combined with that controlled by the Milner Group in other fields—in education, in administration, in newspapers and periodicals—a really terrifying picture begins to emerge."

—Carroll Quigley,
The Anglo-American Establishment

CHAPTER 10

What can we do? What will you do? A forty five step plan.

I wish it were possible for every American Citizen to understand the dangers the United States and indeed that World is facing, but the New World Order programming and mind control is so deep that there are millions that will categorically deny that anything is wrong, especially if it points to our own elected officials. You only have to use the internet search term "**Mark Dice petition for Orwelian Police State**" and you will find an incredible video that shows people signing a petition to introduce an Orwelian Police State, a police state modeled on Russia and Nazi Germany and even people signing a petition to inject children with mercury to help increase autism rates.

They, I'm afraid, must be considered the first victims of the war, they truly are the *walking dead* and once you've identified them you should not waste any more time trying to help them. Instead move on to someone that does have a chance of breaking free of the trance. I fully understand how difficult this can be, especially when you realize that a family member or dear friend falls into that category, but the programming runs so deep in many people that no amount of persuasion will convince them otherwise.

It has been my intention in this book and the previous book to provide people with a concise, uncomplicated and verifiable data showing how we have been manipulated towards a World that by choice we would not desire.

The author of "*Brave New World*", Aldous Huxley once said in a 1962 speech that he gave at U.C. Berkeley

> "A number of techniques about which I talked seem to be here already. And there seems to be a general movement in the direction of this kind of ultimate revolution, a method of control by which a people can be made to enjoy a state of affairs by which any decent standard they ought not to enjoy. This, the enjoyment of servitude, Well this process is, as I say, has gone on for over the years, and I have become more and more interested in what is happening . . . . That if you can get people to consent to the state of affairs in which they're living. The state of servitude, the state of being, having their differences ironed out, and being made amenable to mass production methods on the social level, if you can do this, then you have, you are likely, to have a much more stable and lasting society. Much more easily controllable society than you would if you were relying wholly on clubs and firing squads and concentration camps."

I hope my books can become one tool in the arsenal of the resistance, but that requires every reader and that includes you, to do their part.

Looking the other way and hoping that "they" won't continue with "their" plans will not work this time. Lord Betrand Russell wrote in "The Scientific Outlook" (1931) in a chapter titled "Artificially Created Societies" that:

"submissiveness must be more admired than it has been in the past."

The sword is coming down and the Watchmen are blowing their trumpets.

I will now outline what I believe are the forty five steps that we must take to change our direction. I do not claim ownership to these ideas, I am merely listing, in no particular order, many of the great ideas that better minds have previously outlined.

1. Reinstate the Hearings on Un-American Activities with a clear process to ensure that charges of treason will be levied at any person found to be subverting or undermining the interests of the United States from within.

2. Kick out the Federal Reserve and introduce an amendment to the Constitution that ensures a Central Bank is not allowed to operate in the United States again. The Federal Reserve is the third and most devastating central bank to operate in the US. The Central Banks and the *Banksters* behind them have been the catalyst to moving the *Globalist* agenda forward and they must be stopped.

3. Immediately stop the Fluoridation of our water supply and work to remove Fluoride from toothpaste and other substances (other than rat poison) from public consumption. We have learnt how fluoride was part of the Communist plan to make Americans docile as well as cause cancers and reduce fertility.

4. Demolish the Georgia Guidestones. We do not need this symbol of the globalist and *their* ten commandments. We already have our ten commandments from God and we should be abiding by them.

5. Conduct a thorough investigation into Chemtrails. Identify those responsible for the constant spraying of dangerous chemicals into our atmosphere, uncover the reason why we have been sprayed like bugs for almost two decades. Charge those responsible with treason and crimes against humanity. Those pilots who have knowingly sprayed these chemicals and refuse to provide help or

assistance in tracking down the criminals should also be charged with treason.

6. Conduct a thorough investigation into the events of September 11, 2001. Charges of treason should be brought to all those complicit in this False Flag event.

7. Promote the teaching and meaning of a False Flag attack in schools. This will help future generations understand how the criminal mind works and will help the United States avoid attempts to undermine our society from within.

8. Conduct a thorough investigation into the real background of our President who is currently using the name Barack Obama and if it is found that he is indeed a liar and a fraud he should be immediately impeached and charged accordingly. Any laws passed during his presidency should be immediately repealed.

9. The United States should withdraw from the United Nations and encourage them to leave New York City and the Rockefeller granted land by the use of taxation. Ensure that the United States regains its true status as a sovereign nation and has no legal obligations to bow down to any demand from the U.N.

10. Repeal laws allowing for homo-sexual and lesbian marriage. Re-confirm that the United States only recognizes a marriage between men and women. Discourage the promotion of homo-sexual and lesbian behavior through television and other media.

11. Ban abortions. Anyone conducting abortions should be tried for murder and anyone seeking an abortion should be charged with attempted murder. Planned Parenthood should undergo a major overhaul whereby they focus on teaching moral behavior in children and teenagers, and in helping any unwanted babies find a good caring home.

12. Promote natural healing methods such as regular Chiropractic care, Reiki, homeopathy and acupuncture. Encourage the practice of martial arts and yoga in schools.

13. Stop all immigration until the economic and workforce demands require or allow for an increase. Crackdown on all illegal immigrants by withholding free medical care and other benefits. Deport illegal immigrants to their country of origin.

14. Shutdown the High-Frequency Active Aural Research Program (HAARP) program immediately. HAARP is being used for weather modification, geo-engineering (including the ability to trigger earthquakes) and other nefarious reasons and it has no benefit to humanity.
15. Encourage gun ownership and promote concealed carry. Mandate firearms training for all high school students and all teachers.
16. Convert back to a gold-backed currency and ensure that a fiat currency is never allowed to be created again.
17. Conduct a full banking practices overhaul including illegalize the practice of "Fractional Reserve Banking" which allows banks to leverage ten times the amount of money they have access to and illegalize the use of "Call and Put" options which are essential bets on a future stock price.
18. Severe our "special relationship" with the British Royal family.
19. Conduct an overhaul of the Food and Drug Administration and thoroughly investigate unethical practices and ties to pharmaceutical companies.
20. Implement a complete ban on any pharmaceutical drug that has been linked to or proven to have resulted in death with normal use. Pharmaceuticals should no longer have an option to use a simple profit versus claims loss to determine if a drug can continue to be marketed.
21. Encourage food and water producers through the use of heavy fines or taxes to stop using Bisphenol A in any containers that might come into contact with food or water products.
22. Immediately revise regulations that allow for products such as Aspartame and High Fructose Corn Syrup to be renamed as "natural" products. Promote real nutrition in schools and educate children and adults on the dangers of microwave cookers and other chemical additives and excitotoxins such as M.S.G.
23. Immediately halt the roll out of "Smart Meters" and introduce a program to replace them with devices that do not emit dangerous high frequencies.
24. Nullify and repeal the National Defense Authorization Act (NDAA) which allows American citizens to be detained indefinitely and without charge or a trial.

25. Within a reasonable time conduct a review for the need of the 16th Amendment, which allows Congress to levy income tax. Evidence indicates that this Amendment should not have been passed since it did not legally have enough States to ratify the decision.

26. Encourage companies to bring back manufacturing to the United States by removing tax breaks for off shoring manufacturing or services and offering tax incentives to establish new U.S. based businesses.

27. Conduct a full investigation into Monsanto, Dupont and all other companies who are developing Genetically Modified Foods. Until independent scientific tests proves otherwise the U.S. should repeal any laws that have allowed Genetically Modified plants and animals to be introduced into the food system.

28. Conduct a full scientific and independent assessment of the use of vaccines and the preservatives and adjuvants that are added to them. Vaccines should never be mandated for any reason and laws must be put in place to protect the rights of people such that it becomes their choice alone.

29. Review all current Executive Orders and nullify any orders that circumvents the Constitution.

30. Ensure that Congress has full access and approves plans for Continuity Of Government (C.O.G.)

31. Conduct a safe withdrawal of U.S. Troops from all overseas bases unless Congress has confirmed a State of War exists such that it is necessary to have troops stationed abroad.

32. Repeal the Patriot Act and re-introduce the Posse Comitatus Act to prevent U.S. Military or any Foreign troops from operating within the United States.

33. Promote and encourage "preparedness", especially for those living in natural disaster zones. Citizens should be encouraged to take responsibility for their own long term food and water supply.

34. Immediately withdraw financial and other types of aid to any Communist or any country that cannot be verifiably confirmed as a democratically elected government.

35. Shutdown the Transport and Security Agency (TSA) and replace airport security with privately run companies to be contracted by airline companies.

36. Rebuild our national defenses and our ability to defend the United States.

37. Conduct a full and independent study on the dangers or cell phone technologies and WiFi. Research other safer technologies as a replacement should the study on cell phone and WiFi prove to be undermining human health.

38. Immediately ban the sale of light bulbs containing mercury. The potential impact to human health from a broken light bulb which contains mercury can be devastating and irreversible. Conduct an investigation into the real reason why these light bulbs have an Federal Communications Commission (FCC) logo and ensure that no future light bulbs can be used as a communications device without the understanding of the user.

39. Introduce new legislation that will forever ensure that humans will never be required for any reason to implant a RFID chip or similar such device.

40. Introduce laws and regulations to make it illegal for any person seeking election to State or Federal Government position to be a member of, or have close association with any secret society. Any official found to have such ties should be dismissed and face possible charges of treason.

41. Nullify, repeal and dismiss any regulation or law pertaining to the United Nations Agenda for the Twenty First Century (more commonly known as Agenda 21). Agenda 21 is a key element of the Globalist plans for a *one world government* and should not be permitted to be considered within the United States.

42. Cancel all Central Bank/Federal Reserve created debts and develop a budget that minimizes any debts, especially foreign owned debts.

43. Conduct an overhaul of our education system. Repeal the no child left behind policy. Promote and encourage left and right brain thinking. Promote and encourage music and competitive sports. Teach the concepts of the Constitution and the history of our country and the Founding Fathers struggle for freedom against tyranny. Encourage home schooling.

44. Conduct an overhaul of our election process. Limit contributions from individuals and corporations. Develop procedures to ensure

that no foreign donations can be made. Investigate any claims of under the table deals and prosecute to the full extent of the law.
45. Promote and encourage morality, integrity and a return to strong family traditions. Bring back God.

Of course there is a lot more that we can and should do, but I believe that if we as individuals, families and our elected officials follow these steps or goals then the United States can return to the glory days and be the envy of the entire World.

* * *

What I have included in my two books covers just a small section of the overall Global Conspiracy, but to be honest it was never my intention to detail everything that I have researched. That would have taken many months to produce and who these days will choose to read a book like this that's got more pages than the number of lies told to us by our government. I have though included what I felt was enough to prove my point—that we are being manipulated towards a very grim future, but that with an awakening and the courage to do something, we can change direction.

So with that, I had set out with the hope that one or both of these books would trigger an awakening in those people who are ready to be triggered. Those people that could feel that something was not quite right, but did not know how to fit the pieces of the puzzle together. After several years of trying to do this I fully understand that I will not reach everyone—some people have I have stated before are just not ready, at least not in this lifetime. I understand that one of my life's challenges is to accept that. I do find it very difficult, but I believe I'm winning the battle.

Although I have not mentioned it much in this book I do want to add that it was not my intention to scare anyone or create any fear. If you do go on to research more about the *conspiracy*, you will learn that our planet is ruled by satanic worshiping *entities* that feed off our fear as well as using it as a control mechanism. We must not feed them. Let go of your fear, let in and send out love—they really don't like that.

The controllers also understand that if they can keep you in fear then they know you will not rise up and resist them—well I say NO FEAR, JUST LOVE and now get out there and resist and do what you can to wake others up!

For those wanting more information to research here's a small list of topics that I've either not mentioned or have just covered in limited detail:

HAARP

Agenda 21

Child Kidnapping rings and Pedophilia

Our Holographic World—Specifically books and videos by David Icke

Lost civilizations—the work by Graham Hancock is very good on this subject

Chemtrails

The Bilderberg Group—see reference to Daniel Estulin's book

The history of the Round Table and Milner Group—If you are up to the task Carroll Quigley's "Tragedy and Hope" and "The Anglo-American Establishment" will fit the bill.

The history of the Royal Institute of International Affairs and the Council on Foreign Relations—as per note above.

Bibliography

1. NATIONAL SECURITY PRESIDENTIAL DIRECTIVE/NSPD 51
2. The United States Civil Disturbance Plan 55-2
3. U.S. Military Civil Disturbance Planning: The War at Home, Frank Morales, P 1
4. FM 3-39.40 Internment and Resettlement Operations, Department of the Army, February 2010 Section 1-19
5. Ibid, Sect 1-20
6. Ibid, Sect 3-56
7. Ibid, Appendix K-24
8. FM 3-19.15 Civil Disturbance Operations. Department of the Army, April 2005, 7-13
9. Army Regulation 210-35 Civilian Inmate Labor Program, Summary
10. Ibid, 1-5
11. Ibid, 2-3
12. Journey to a Brave New World, P114
13. Ibid, Chapter 4
14. Ibid, P31
15. Ibid, P12
16. Bertrand Russell, "The Scientific Outlook", 1931 P 211
17. Ibid P215
18. Joel M. Skousen, Strategic Relocation, 3rd Edition P 34
19. Ibid, P36

20. Stanislav Lunev, "Through the Eyes of the Enemy" P 22-31
21. Craig Roberts, The Medusa File, P353
22. Edward Bernays, "Propaganda", 1928 Cover
23. Carroll Quigley, "The Anglo-American Establishment", P197
24. Ibid, P139
25. W. Cleon Skousen, The Naked Communist, 1958, P258
26. Ibid, P259-262
27. Carroll Quigley, Tragedy and Hope, P331
28. Gary Allen, The Rockefeller File, Chapter 10
29. John Holdren, Paul Ehrlich, Anne Ehrlich, "Ecoscience—Population, Resources, Environment" (1977)P786
30. Daniel Estulin, "The True Story of the Bilderberg Group", P180
31. Paul Kengor Ph.D. "The Communist" (2012) P4

OTHER SOURCES:

1. FEDBIZOPS.GOV
2. Police State:2000 DVD by Alex Jones
3. Police State 4: the Rise of FEMA, DVD by Alex Jones
4. Dreams from my real father, DVD by Joel Gilbert
5. No Place to Hide—the Strategy and Tactics of Terrorism—Documentary film 1982, Western Goals Foundation
6. The Obama Deception, DVD by Alex Jones
7. Agenda—Grinding America Down, DVD
8. Powerderburns, Cocaine, Contras & the Drug War, Celerino Castillo III with Dave Harmon
9. 9/11 Road to Tyranny, DVD by Alex Jones
10. United Nations Arms Trade Treaty